Programming For Data Science

2 Books in 1

Cyber Security, SQL Programming, Beginners Course for Kids, and Newbies (Crash Course 2021)

Cyber

Security

Learn All the Essentials and Basic Ways to Avoid Cyber Risk for Your Business (Cyber security Guide for Beginners)

Ben Chan

Table of content

Introduction

In a world where safety is a top priority, we have to make it a point of reference to safeguard what is rightfully ours. Many understand the importance of cyber security, while others, not so much, but your level of understanding of the importance of cyber security does not increase or decrease its relevance, neither does it make it more or less important.

What is Cybercrime?

The term cybercrime defines criminal activities that involve the use of a computer and the internet.

What is Cybersecurity?

Cyber security, on the other hand, is the art of defending your computer as well as any of your devices and data from any attacks from cybercriminals.

Many companies in the U.S. lose about $525 million annually, which goes to show the importance of having adequate cyber security to tackle the level of cybercrime we have today. One might care to think that they target only the big guns, which means that some of the small companies and SMEs are out of it. If you are in this category of people, then I have to tell you that you are mistaken because cybercrime is random and unpredictable, leaving everyone at risk of being hit.

The internet at inception was looked upon as something that would drive innovation and make the world a better place; yes, this is true. But with every good thing comes those who would try to exploit from the other side. At whatever level you find yourself, cyber security is a must if you want to secure yourself as well as your business from the peril of cybercrime.

In this book, we are going to look at cybersecurity as a whole and how it can be used to secure your business today. Cybercrime has become popular today and has become a part of the digital world. The cybercrimes we are talking about here are growing daily and with the growth comes more loss and sophistication. Many of these cybercriminals target the critical side of the infrastructure of many countries looking to cause havoc in any way they can. Many other cybercriminals, like identity thieves, target the average citizens and many other criminal situations.

With every passing day we are experiencing new cybercrimes, and the prevalence of this problem is increasing with the occurrence of social media. From the inception of social media till the year 2020, the cybercrime stats have grown to $1.5 trillion and are still on the rise. As we move on, we are going to be looking at some of the cybercriminal statistics in a bid to convince you of not just the prevalence of the problem but also the need for you to take action.

For many organizations and businesses, the prevalence of cybercrime is on the increase, and it does not simply have an impact on the financial aspect of their business but also, the side which points to their level of reliability, and their reputation – something which took them a lot of time to build.

- The cybercrime industry, in general, costs businesses a total of $1.5 trillion as of 2018.
- The introduction of social media helped cybercriminals generate about $3.5 billion in global revenue yearly.
- Also, social media caused the sale of stolen personal data, which was worth about $640 million every year.
- The majority of the economy of cybercrime involves the use of bitcoin.

- The most common type of cybercrime in many organizations is malware attacks.
- Email phishing scams are top priority risks that are growing rapidly.
- The FBI receives more than 300,000 calls related to cybercrime every year.
- The preferred victims of cybercriminals are individuals who are over the age of 60, as they are known to be more susceptible to deceit.
- A quarter of malware attacks targeted financial companies like banks.
- The cybercrimes in Japan, as well as the U.K., rose by a whopping 35% in 2018.

In this book, we are going to be covering the basics of cybersecurity as well as how you can protect yourself from the increasing menace of cybercrime which is continuously on the increase. In the end, you would not only have an understanding of the way they work, but you would also understand how to protect yourself as well as your business and family.

Chapter 1

The Fundamentals of Cyber Security

For everything that is worth discussing, the first essential that needs to be covered is the fundamentals. The fundamentals of cyber security are important if we want to understand the concept and how we can use it to make your company and as well as your personal data safe from theft.

The Concepts of Network and Security

The necessary tools that can be used by business designers to maintain their system security with regards to integrity as well as other important factors are authentication, nonrepudiation, and authorization. Having a good understanding of the concepts of network and security and how they come together to make your system secure. They come together to make sure your system is safe and secure, and without one of these concepts, your security can be left in great peril.

There are three major components that protect your information, known as the CIA triad, which must be understood by anyone who wishes to protect his system from cyber criminals must come to understand. These concepts are confidentiality, integrity, and availability.

Many of the professionals who understand this concept are devoted to making sure that they protect the information on every system. So, this chapter covers the basics, and as we move on, we are not going to indulge in any complexities as we are simply going to go straight to the point with all the aspects of what we need to cover.

What do we mean by this? We simply mean that we are covering all levels of attack, as well as some of the things you can do to protect yourself and your business from these points of attack.

Points of Attack

- Your computer files – the files on your computer can be a very big point of attack for cybercriminals who wish to target the information you have and use it against you.

- Email scams – we are also going to be covering email scams and how you can discern which information is true and which is false.
- Malware intrusion – this is where you need to guide against unauthorized access to your devices as malware can do this.
- Information security – another important aspect of cybersecurity.
- Security for your Wi-Fi – Wi-Fi can be used to hack you as well as your system, so you need to know how to secure your Wi-Fi as well.
- Connecting a new P.C. to the internet – avoiding attacks and intrusion from the get-go.
- Internet scams – important information on how to protect your computer from internet scams.
- Securing your home network – your home network is a likely intrusion point, and if you do not protect it, you are likely to regret it.
- Securing your web browser – as simple as a web browser is, it can cost you dearly.
- Virus basics – all you need to know about viruses and how you can protect yourself.

After the basics, we are going to be covering other essentials with regards to getting a safer working environment for yourself as well as your business.

This book is strategically designed to get you past basically every aspect of cybercrime and how you can scale past them with ease.

Securing Your Files

As a computer user, whether on a professional basis or as a home user looking to stay safe from the terrors of cybercrime, you need to understand the importance of securing your files, and one of the best ways to do this is by securing your data and files. You should understand that backing up the files and data you have on your laptop, mobile phones, or desktop is very important to protect them from loss or cybercrime. For you to really safeguard your devices, it is not enough to have a backup folder on your device, but rather, it is best that you do the following so you can have the best chance of recovering your stolen or corrupted data.

- Make sure you have up to 3 copies of all your essential files saved in your primary and backup folder.

- Make sure these backups are saved on at least two different media types to prevent a total loss.
- Make sure one of these files is saved somewhere safe and apparently not at your home or business location.

Moving forward, we are going to be looking at the different backup locations as well as the advantages and disadvantages of saving information at these backup locations.

Cloud Storage

With the increase of the internet broadband, cloud storage has become available to many users, and this shared puddle of computing is owned by your cloud service provider of choice, giving you access to store your information as you want.

Pros

- Cloud storage helps you save you data even in the worst-case scenarios such as natural disasters, and damaged devices.
- Full access to your information irrespective of your location.

- The cloud space you purchase would specifically be according to your needs in terms of space.

Cons

- The cloud is heavily dependent on the internet, which can sometimes cause a delay between you and your data, so sometimes; you might get stranded for a while due to server issues.

Internal HDD

Your hard disk drive makes use of a spinning magnetic salver to store your information. Virtually every computer makes use of this HDD for storing information. This is also used by secondary systems for storing vital information. The hard disk capacity you buy is dependent on the information you want to store as well as your choice.

Pros

- Easy updates of files since your main and backup files are stored on the same internal file. With this, you make an update and maintain the original file structure.

Cons

- Easy loss of data via theft, malware, or corruption of the hard disk - bad way to lose all your files.

Removable Storage Media

This is a simple and easy to use storage device which you can connect and disconnect from your device whenever you want to store information. This storage gives you the chance to store your information away from your device, keeping it safe from theft and damages.

Pros

- Very easy to work with as you can move them from one place to the other without any prior issues.
- They are available in many sizes and capacities, all of which can fit your budget.

Cons

- Prone to loss, as many of them are very portable.
- It has the capacity to corrupt the entire system as well as the information on it.

Chapter 2

Malware and Cyber attacks

The consistent attacks on our cyberspace have increased rapidly, and more so with the help of malware which has caused many individuals as well as companies to check out what is going on with the cyberspace and how they can protect themselves moving forward. The malware produced today has far overpowered the traditional antimalware strategies which have been used over time, making it easy for cybercriminals to perpetuate their criminal actions while companies and individuals are finding it difficult to cope with these criminal activities.

This chapter will enlighten you on the topic of malware, what makes them such a big threat to you and your company and the part they play in many of the modern attacks that people face today.

What are the main characteristics of this advanced Malware?

This signature-based anti-virus software is one that many teams have been trying to fight for many years with little success to show for their stress. The reason for this is that the majority of the traditional detection software takes a long while, mostly more than six months before any malware is detected. This has given the malware enough time to get the damage done. These malwares capitalize on system vulnerabilities known as bugs or flaws which are available in system software, giving the cyber attacker full access to the system. The attacker then crafts an entry point and, from there, the weaknesses of the software, thereby deceiving the software into taking actions which the attacker wants.

Looking at the time which this malware takes before detection, there are some factors we need to consider:

- The attacker has the ability to detect the anti-malware software available on the system, which is then used to update the antimalware software such that it becomes almost impossible to detect.

- There is specialized malware that is designed for specific businesses and organizations, making it almost impossible to detect since it is specifically designed to prey on the defects of that particular software.

- Other advanced software takes the host software as prey, updating and advancing as the days go by. This malware is updated as they go, and whenever there is a roadblock, it is simply updated again to cross the blockade, gaining more access to vital and important information.

If you notice, the malware we have now compared to those which we had before are simply different. What has changed? Well, cybercriminals have shifted from the times of doing things randomly down to the point where they have become well-co-ordinated, targeting specific organizations with malware specifically designed to drill information and data out of specific organizations. The internet has taken a turn with positive developments giving everyone access to personal and unlimited possibilities.

If an organization is attacked by more than a single software, the possibility of this malware coming together to work towards a common goal is infinite. Even with many malware designed and inputted into an organizational software, they can come together working cohesively for all the attackers. Looking at advanced malware, here are some of the capabilities, and features:

Polymorphism: many of the anti-malware programs make use of hash signatures for the detection of the source code of every file in the system. This code can be edited and changed, thereby changing the entire hash signature of the code, but this cannot be done anytime there is a suspicion that the current detection of the anti-malware software. However, polymorphism makes this possible since the hash signatures of the malware are constantly changed, leaving even the simplest of malware programs undetectable.

Resistant Architecture: advanced malware takes full advantage of the internet and the flexibility that comes with it. There are many servers which the internet uses for its sustainability, and this is also used by this advanced malware, which allows it to remain in total functionality, even where there are challenges with system fight backs. This also gives this malware access to other affected points on the system, which can almost lead to total access.

Multiple Capabilities: advanced malware is not designed for specific tasks only as they can be edited and updated from control centers changing the functionality in the process. This capability gives the attacker permission to carry out different actions depending on the needs per time.

Confusion technique: many of the new and advanced malware confuses anti-malware software by hiding the usual binary strings used by usual malware software. This is achieved using sophisticated algorithms to compress the program during the time of entry and then decompress when it is time to run. This way, the malware looks like something else to the anti-malware software, giving it an easy pass when trying to detect.

A Closer Look at Modern Strategies Used for Cyberattacks

The strategies used for modern cyberattacks have changed drastically. Compared to attack strategies used beforehand, the strategies used to cover cyber-attacks are more technical, detailed, and specific. For an attacker to specifically say he wants to target a high-profile system, a couple of steps need to be taken, and this is something we are going to be looking at in this section.

For a cyber-attacker to successfully attack a system, here are some of the steps they take:

Investigation: it's just like when criminals rob a bank. They do not just choose random banks, but the ones they have access to and can easily define their security system and can define how to infiltrate. Cybercriminals, however, make use of tools such as phishing, fake email address marketing, and many more. They make use of other tools to search the system for weaknesses as well as application problems that can be exploited.

Arming and Delivery: at the point when reconnaissance is completed, the next line of action is determining the sort of malware that would fit the software as well as the mode of delivery. If the web page of the target is the chosen point of action, it can be exploited and used to target the vulnerability in the system software. At the point where the advanced malware gets into the system, it gets in without the knowledge of the user.

Exploitation: when it comes to exploitation, the cybercriminal typically has two options:

- Making use of social points where a user is tricked into clicking a link that opens a malicious file.

- Option two talks about software exploits, which has to do with deceiving the user software, application, or web browser to run a malicious code that was developed by the attacker. This is to say that the attacker develops a malware based on the vulnerabilities of the user system.

Once the system has been fully exploited, the advanced malware has been fully installed, giving the cyber-criminal full access to the system. This method has become efficient for many cyber-criminals, basically because it goes unnoticed by the system. This has become more efficient and popular for cybercriminals because of the simplification of this software. All it takes is the right tools and the patience to match as the technicality is about one of the least skills required to make this happen.

Installation: once the advance malware has completely entered into the system, it is now necessary for the attacker to make sure that the malware would stick. Here are some of the advanced malware used for this purpose:

Bootkits: this rootkit is a kernel variant, used for attacking computers protected with encryptions.

RootKit: this is a special malware that gives the attacker root-level access to the computer.

Backdoors, however, allows the attacker to move past the usual authentication process so he can gain access to the system. It is often installed as a failover system just in case a system detects the presence of malware and then removes it from the system.

There is also the installation of Anti-AV software which is installed specifically to remove any antivirus system on the user endpoint. This works to prevent the detection and removal of any installed malware installed by the cybercriminal. How does this Anti-AV system work? By simply infecting the master boot record of the target system, making malware virtually undetectable.

Command and Control: for a cyberattack to be successful there must be communication between the attacker and the endpoint. The cybercriminal should be able to communicate with the system which is infected and, in the process, take hold of the information which he wants to get in the first place. With this information, the cybercriminal has the capacity to move without being noticed, such that he has the capacity to target other systems in the target system. Therefore, if the system is attacked, the point of entry is just the first point of attack. If the attacker needs to get some more information at other points, he can move towards the ultimate goal, which is the main reason for hacking in the first place.

This communication line must be stealthy in such a way that it would not raise any suspicion from the end-user in the first place. This is not an easy technique but rather one which includes the process which we are about to highlight:

Encryption making use of SSH, SSL as well as any other custom application. The most common type of encryption used by hackers is the proprietary encryption. One of the major tools used by hackers is the BitTorrent application, which has excellent proprietary encryption and is used by hackers for infecting the host system as well as continuous communication.

• Evasion via the use of protocols, tunneling applications in applications, proxies, and remote desktop access tools.

• Another method is the port evasion which makes use of port hopping to tunnel over open ports, as well as anonymizers for networks.

• Finally, fast flux to the proxy via many infected hosts, and then make it hard for their team to comprehend where the traffic is going to.

• Action: there might be a thousand reasons why the attacker decided to hit the target computer, and for whatever reason it is, this last step talks about action. This phase lasts for a long while, depending on the action strategy of the cybercriminal. For some, fast and straightforward is the way, while for others, a slow attack is a right thing to do. Irrespective of the plan, the end result is an attack without eventual detection.

Security Factors and opportunities

Even with the level of sophistication these cybercriminals show, there are still some loopholes in their game, many of which we would like to highlight.

Some of the loopholes we would like to enlighten you on are as follows:

For an attack to function properly there must be a communication channel.

The threat of cyber-attacks today is one that works based on communication. This communication network pattern requires that there be a channel of communication between you and the system which is being attacked. Once this is the case there is one thing that can be done, and that is to neutralize the communication line. Once this can be done, the threat is largely non-existent from this point.

There are many opportunities to detect and compare.

Looking at the attack lifecycle we highlighted in this section from start to finish, one fact is sure, and that is that there are multiple steps involved from the start to the finish of an attack. The number of steps here, therefore, points to the fact that there are multiple chances to not only identify but also counter the threats.

The major source of concern should be the framework of the threat.

Once the cybercriminal has access to the target, communicate consistently, and manage the affairs of the target system, then there is no limit to what can be achieved. This is to say that once the cyber attacker has control over the target system; your primary concern should be facing the attack. It is only when this is done that you can stop the target on its tracks. Look at the attack as a framework rather than a simple hit and move payload.

The diversity of your security must match the sophistication of threats.

For many companies and users looking to put an end to the menace of cyberattacks, their first line of action is advanced endpoint protection, firewalls, content filtering. These have been the elite protection strategies overtime when it comes to security, but these traditional methods have not stood the test of time when getting to face the challenge of new attacks such as the following:

• Files: these have been used to steal data as well as update malware.

• URLs and Websites: these are endpoints for hosting and enabling new threats.

• Applications: these are points that threaten the system while hiding in plain sight.

• Exploits: this formulates shell access to the target, which at some point changes or rather improves access to the target system.

• Malware: this takes control of the target system, and in the process, compromises the system.

Your security must go past the usual points to include the endpoint, the cloud environment as well as your network

As an organization, there is a need to increase your point of focus as these criminals know how you think and have looked for other means beyond your usual scope. You have to improve your scope of vision, both inward and outward. This is only accomplished by simply making use of the new and up to date security platforms, which can help you enforce within and outside the network traffic.

Chapter 3

Traditional security Vs. Advanced Malware

The treat which is faced today on the front of cyber terrorism is something that has gone through stages upon stages of development. Is it, therefore, possible that your security protocols which have remained the same over time would be able to detect, let alone comprehend with the latest levels of threat that are out there? It is only logical to see this as an almost impossible task to accomplish. The traditional intrusion prevention systems, firewalls, as well as other known methods, do not cut it any longer.

As we move on in this chapter, we are going to be looking at this advanced malware further and how it has challenged the traditional security protocols as well as its ability to protect you from the attacks that have seemingly been revolutionized. I believe that as we go further, we are going to understand the strengths of this advanced malware as well as where our systems are lacking in terms of the level of security that they offer. This section taken seriously because when light is shone on a situation, there is reason to believe in the possibility of a solution.

Rapidly Growing Attack vectors

Looking at the state of attacks by cybercriminals in the past, where the simple line of action was to target the end users via email, there were simple and effective ways to handle coming threats. This was because there was a single point of entry known to everyone. At some point, moving forward due to the revolution of the technology sector, there is now a countless number of ways in which cybercriminals attack their end-users with the use of many other applications. These ways have changed the scope of the attack, and some of them are:

- Software as a Service (SaaS) application.

- Microsoft office – surprising right! I know.

- Multiple social media platforms – Facebook, Instagram, twitter.

- Organizational emails, as well as webinars.

- File transfer app.

- Workflow and collaboration applications.

- Instant messaging

I'm sure there are some of these ways you are not surprised about, and there are many others you never expected to be on this list. This goes to show that those people attacking you, as well as your businesses, have many points of entry. To make matters even more complicated, these applications seem more legit than some of the legit applications you know – I know right! The scam looking better than the legit, sometimes they can make more money than they think they could, if they would go legit. It is difficult to notice email delays as messages are inspected for malware on an email server preceding delivery. At the moment, threats are streamed, making use of browsers as well as many other platforms which, if delayed at some point, would lead to widespread complaints from users.

A lack of logical end-to-end visibility

As we know, a cyberattack is a well-orchestrated set of tools with vast capabilities. Security solutions that are distinct and used for specific reasons do not cut it at this point. These security systems do not have the ability to communicate with other systems, thereby isolating a part of the system. This isolation can, therefore, open other systems to many threats and an eventual attack. You can liken this to a security system with just two guards in a big building with no communication lines. After reconnaissance, the criminal simply gets to know the loopholes in the security protocols and then attacks. If you look at it this way, you would see that this does not cut it security wise.

For you to make the most of the use and accessibility of applications, many of the new applications are specifically designed to fault the traditional firewalls simply by changing the line of communication. This is a trend that has been taken up by much advanced malware and used to get access to the systems of many users. This is true because the threats you cannot see cannot be tackled, and you have to know that advanced malware makes use of a lot of tricks that hide the true nature of their network. Some of the tricks used to hide their endpoint include the following:

• Obfuscation and encoding: the transmission of malware is always encoded in a special way. The process of obfuscation and encoding does not just help to prevent detection, but also helps to hide the true reason for the malware intrusion in the first place. This is simple for the malware as all it has to do is convert the simple strings into developed and complicated algorithms.

• Proxies: cybercriminals make use of proxies to cross the usual firewalls. This allows the malware access to making an anonymous network while it protects its communication. This hides the malware while it goes through the system, conducting numerous activities.

• Circumventors and Anonymizers: these are applications specially built to avoid detection by network security controls. Unlike other infiltrations, these anonymizers have no open or genuine use on company networks. These applications are updated monthly for the process of avoiding detection by the system's traditional means of recollection.

• Tunneling: the method of tunneling helps attackers hide their malicious activities. These protocols and activities support the attacker with the ability to send data and information via the public network inside other applications that are in use on the network. This method allows the covering of their communication rather as applications and services that are allowed on the network, which gives then access to the system and a way beyond the usual perimeter that is set by the security protocols of the system.

• Port hopping and non-standard ports: the port-based firewalls set by users are easily evaded by the use of evasive applications. However, threat products and IPS also rely on the use of ports to determine which analysis and signatures to apply to traffic. These weaknesses are then made obvious by the fact that APTs (Advanced Persistent Threats) are interconnected from the inside of the infected network back to the attacker outside of the system. This allows full access to the attacker as well as the flexibility to make use of the port and protocols as he deems fit. This does not only grant access but also overthrows any process which is against port-based controls.

• SSL (Secure Sockets Layer) encryption: many of the cybercriminals who create malware rely massively on different types of encryptions to hide their different types of command and control traffic linked with the installed malware. One of the most sought methods is the SSL encryption because this is one of the default protocols for many social media platforms such as

Facebook. These sites are popular in use, making them one of the best places for malware delivery. Due to the use of this SSL encryption, many security teams find it hard to see malware traffic on their network. There are other encryptions that make this possible such as the peer-to-peer applications which infect and then take control of the system, allowing attackers to control the system, allowing their content and commands pass through the system firewall without detection.

On a final note, many new businesses also make use of these methods to improve the ease at which they operate while reducing the rate of disturbance for clients, customers, and partners services as such. An example of this is Skype. Skype makes use of port hopping because it is an important aspect of their application functionality rather than as a means to avoid detection or improve server accessibility generally.

Avoiding hash-based signatures

The simple approach used for spotting and blocking off malware is based on the idea that the method of collecting malware and creating a firewall that would specifically block the access of that malware. Even though this seems like one of the best approaches to take, there are several problems which would be faced when making use of this method, such as:

- A long wait before completion.

- High operational cost.

By design, this protection system which is created cannot be used until the malware is inside the system. Trying to do this is like trying to make use of a vaccine without the patient being infected. In the process of waiting for this protection firewall to be finished and with the malware already in the system, the system is already susceptible to threats from different angles. It is just like handing the keys to a criminal who has been trying to rob your apartment for months.

For your network to be protected from some of these attackers, a new and active malware ought to be caught by your system before a detection and protection signature can be made by your IT engineers. This signifies that as a user, you would be breached and on the verge of losing valuable information until the time of detection and eventually detection signature is created and then enforced. This means that attackers have all the free time in the world to do what they want with your systems as well as your network. This malware is something that is new for every organisation, and it is safe to say that another reason for late detection is the lack of communication between customers and the company.

This lack of communication line has been taken to the next level by the new and advanced malware today and has expanded upon it, by new and developing techniques to avoid being spotted, by all means, avoiding signatures that have been created as well as from detecting them. All of this can point to the fact that, these new advanced malware systems are dynamic, which gives them the chance to fit into any system of choice, just like a chameleon, which changes its colour to blend into the environment and avoid capture in the process. As we go into the next section, we are going to talk about polymorphism as well as targeted malware, which is another technique used to evade the strengths of signature-based detection systems put up by companies and businesses online.

Targeted Malware

Before the advancement of malware, making it a global network threat, the ideal objective of malware on a network was simply infecting a system and replicating it. The success or failure of a malware system was dependent on whether it could replicate very fast and within what period of time was this replication. This made it easily and readily available for collection, which meant that at some point, with the widespread of malware, the detection was easy, and the eventual collection made it easy to create a firewall around the system.

This is not the case anymore as the new and advanced malware systems have changed their model of attack. This malware is more dynamic and intelligent, allowing cybercriminal access to navigate and control the subject system, and as at this point, having many users who are infected is not the endgame. Once the attacker has the target user in sight, the rest is history as the objective has been reached and infiltrated.

In these kinds of situations, we can say that attackers have changed from making simple rampart malware to targeted ones, specifically designed to infiltrate and attack a particular user. With this approach, there are two important things which are accomplished:

1. This makes it almost unlikely that the malware would be detected and caught since they target specific users rather than random millions of users globally.

2. It is evasive, which means that it is designed to avoid networks which they are not meant for. With this system, it means that you can only get hit if you are the target, making detection difficult.

Usual Network controls are ineffective

Many of the usual network system solutions were designed to cover the problems of the old and replicating malware rather than the new and advanced malware systems. Many of the old systems have detection bases, which mean that once they spot it, then they move to block or contain it. For the advanced systems which are dynamic in nature, there is a lot more work to do. This threat can simply bond to an unexpected port, get into the system, and move through without detection. Here are some of the traditional network controls in details:

Firewalls

Many of the port-based firewalls are the usual defense systems, sort of like the fence before the security. This firewall acts as a filter for traffic, segmenting the network into different zones that are protected by passwords. One major problem with this network is the use of ports and protocols to detect the things that get in and out of the systems. This design has one foundation, and this is inefficient when you have an advanced malware which has the capacity to move from one port to the other till the mission is complete. This goes to show how ineffective these firewalls are when it comes to identifying and controlling this advanced malware.

Many have noticed this ineffectiveness and have decided to systems like the Unified Threat Management would not only help them detect but likewise capture the malware, but this was far from right as the system suffered from more attacks due to the poor accuracy in detection, and severe degradation.

Intrusion Prevention Systems

The use of IPSs helps to tackle some of the major challenges of cyber-attacks. This looks deeper into the traffic that comes into a system much more than the usual firewall everyone puts up. So, since we know this, we can still highlight that IPS solutions do not completely run a complete set of signatures on every traffic that comes into the system. What the IPS is designed to do rather is to apply specific signatures to different types of traffics based on ports. This goes to show that when a non-standard port goes through the system, it is likely to be missed by the system. Looking at another limitation, IPS does not have the power of exploit detection needed to cover networks. There are only a couple of exploits, and that is, which is short of the thousands of signatures they need to cover.

Effective IPS makes use of signatures based on exploits, a method which can yield quick results within its capacity, but limited cover if you really check out what it does. We can say that the IPS can provide protection for a long time for many organizations and their infrastructure, but most of the time and in the new and uncommon territory, this might not be the case.

Proxies

Talking about proxies, we are looking at network traffic control from another perspective. Even with the other side which this security protocol handles, we can say that this is also limited to a part of the network traffic, which is to be monitored. Proxies are designed to copy the applications they are trying to monitor, which is why they scuffle to put up with the changes that come when apps are updated as well as with new apps. This is to show that proxies lack the power of protocol support, which is needed since they only understand a few protocols. A final challenge with proxy solutions is data performance, which is inefficient because of the way in which proxy terminates an application and then sends it over to the target destination.

Endpoint Protection

The initial target of hackers looking to get into an organization is known as an endpoint. This is because of the relative vulnerability it has, which is due to the variety of software as well as versions they run on. This diversity makes way for an entry point to the system network as well as access to the information which the cybercriminal wants. Endpoint protection such as anti-virus software has the same challenges as the major signature-based technology, and with this, the only malware that can be detected is the one which is known which means that for the unknown and the new, detection is improbable making it ineffective to these sorts of threats. Also, for users who make use of mobile devices and laptops, they have no IPS or firewall. This simply means that once they are connected to the network of the organization, they act as open points, opening the organization to attacks when they make use of these networks remotely.

Cloud and virtual protection

Since the adoption of cloud computing strategies and virtualization, security solutions must take out time to evolve even more than the cybercriminal community if protection is still going to be a possibility. Within the private cloud, port-based firewalls that are deployed at the perimeter of the network only have a visibility of 60% or even less, which means that cybercriminals have the capacity to move literally through the network without any fear of detection.

Platform as a Service (PaaS), Infrastructure as a Service (IaaS), and Software as a Service (SaaS) are all public cloud environments which have created new attack vectors. The Software as a Service (SaaS) platforms like salesforce and Google Docs have become popular for use by many organizations, and the popularity has made it an entry point for many cybercriminals to gain access to the organizations they have in mind. These SaaS applications are great options for companies as they need only minimal resources in terms of infrastructure for the company, and this is one major reason for the growing popularity. Yet, since these companies and businesses do not have full control of these apps, these apps can be used as entry points by attackers to deliver and spread malware as well as steal vital information.

We have new hybrid cloud environments, which are the combination of private and public cloud environments, and this only implies that we find security solutions that simply must be deployed tactically to address both private and public attack vectors so there can be complete protection of the data in organizations.

You must remember that for effective security, the policies used must be based on both the application in use as well as the identity of users compared to the use of protocols, ports, and IP addresses. Without the full knowledge of the sort of applications used to access the network as well as the identity of users, it is safe to say that most networks would continue to be by-passed by threats if the only source of protection is the use of port-based network controls.

Security Silos

The deficiencies in port-based firewalls have been something organizations have been battling with for a long time now. These deficiencies have been battled simply by implementing many other additional security devices like standalone appliances and other host-based solutions.

Host-based approaches versus the network approach

Most of the time, many organizations have focused their fight against malware on the side of the network or end-user in the form of anti-viruses (host-based) as well as personal viruses. Looking at the evolution of malware, from infected endpoints to the organised malware we have today, organizations need to step up their game by incorporating endpoint and network-level intelligence and controls, moving with data flow, in an approach to be more secure. We can say that network security has more advantages as it allows you to focus on the qualities that separate the old malware of the early days from the new and advanced malware we have now. This is key because for you to say that your network is safe, it has to operate on the same or even a higher level than the advanced malware we have out there.

Also, new mechanisms for network security provide us with a fresh scope for monitoring and controlling our networks as cybercasts the host rime evolves and expands into new vectors. Many of the advanced malware can gain access to undermine the protection you get from your antivirus. This issue creates a problem for security teams because once the software is running on a host that is compromised, then, there is no assured outcome. This does not mean that the security of the host is outdated, but rather it shows that the combined threats against the network, as well as the host, would require a network that takes advantage of the strengths of the network and the host's security measures.

Making use of multidisciplinary solutions

Reducing and eventually stopping the terror of cybercrime necessitates a combined multidisciplinary approach for detecting malicious traffic, connect events, and respond consequently in the network.

Many companies and businesses have deployed many security solutions as an addition to their usual firewall, proxy servers, and antivirus gateways such as email security and instant messaging as a means to improve their defenses against the threats which have increasingly become a problem.

However, this combined approach to security infrastructure brings out new problems such as the following:

- ✓ The performance is stressed due to the high aggregate latency because every traffic goes through scanning on different systems.
- ✓ There are problems with putting information together, and the context between events is lost due to the fact that every security solution is spread into different positions.
- ✓ Inspection requirements, policy management, and access control rules are spread into the different platforms and devices, making it difficult to implement a single and consistent security policy that would fit into every criterion.

Not everything that needs to go through inspection actually does simply because this solution relies on the same port and protocol-based classification as the port-based firewall or because the solution cannot get to see all the traffic that is coming in.

The implementation of more security appliances does not relatively mean more security. It just means you have just taken out time to make your system more complex than it ought to be. With the implementation of this complex security system, it is almost certain that you have put your system's security at risk. What do I mean by this? This system is more cumbersome and complicated, and with this complication comes the difficulty of analysis. Once you find it difficult to analyze, some things might have slipped through without the consent of your team which means more work to do and little less accomplished. In order words bringing together many isolated single-function security systems together can increase the chances of cyberattacks specifically because it opens up more gaps.

Cybersecurity is important today.

Chapter 4

What Is the Way Forward for Security?

From what we have discussed in previous chapters, it is obvious that the security systems we used to have are predominantly stressed and not in any way ready to tackle the problems of cyberattacks. Next-generation security, on the other hand, provides you with perhaps the most important security weapon against the rapidly advancing malware systems. This, however, has its perks and would not work as well as it ought to if it is used in segregation. These advanced next-generation security protocols would fail to provide you with the control and malware visibility that is required in this time and age of online insecurity. To put this all together, if all the available threats are not analyzed, your organisation cannot be well protected.

So, what do we classify as next-generation security?

Next-generation firewall

Once you can take a look at and understand the full spectrum of the available traffic on your network, you can then understand how you can control the traffic coming in as well as the techniques used by malware to gain access to your system. For cyberattacks to function effectively there must be communication. For you to track these advanced malware systems, it only takes you tracking the communication lines, which is an important part of controlling these cybercriminals and the threats they bring to the table. Compared to the old firewalls used these new and advanced firewalls do not make use of port and protocols for traffic classification, but rather a continuous process of heuristics, decoding, decrypting, and application analysis. The capacity for a system to decrypt and identify even the oddest of traffic without the use of any encryption whatsoever is the very definition of a next-generation firewall, something which is more than useful in the fight against cyber threats and advanced malware.

One obvious trait with many cybercriminals is their capacity to blend in with the usual traffic, and your ability to go through every one of that traffic that moves through your network is a priceless gift. It is an important asset every company must possess apart from your ability to go through the traffic that comes in; this firewall gives you access to a threat prevention scheme which is a real representation of co-ordination of multiple security schemes wrapped in one sweet package such as:

- Malware and exploit detection

- Intrusion prevention

- File control

- Content checks

- Application identity

All of these functions together compared to the method of co-locating them in the same hemisphere. The integration of all these functions provides you with a definitive and clear understanding of the working precepts of cybercriminals and malware than individual technology can give to you. This would allow you to see and understand the significant signs of unidentified threats.

How do you prevent infection using this next-generation firewall?

As a business, one of the first steps you need to take is to reduce the risk of attacks and, in turn, control the risk of infection from advanced malware. The majority of vectors used by malware today are basically unchecked, and this happens because of the small size of this malware, which blends into the usual traffic that goes into the network. When you find a way to get full visibility of your network and to control whatever goes through the network, you and your security team have the chance to regain access to your network security once again.

Reducing the attacking field

One of the ways to reduce the attack surface is simply by implementing positive control. When you have implemented positive control, you have reduced the surface of attack, reducing the overall risk you ought to have faced. For many organizations who have tried other methods of control, positive control is the best way to gain control of your network, as it means you have the power to dictate the type of traffic that goes through your network. It also means allowing specific types of applications to get through your network rather than going through the stress of trying to block everything that comes the way of your network.

In terms of security, positive control has been one of the defining factors of network firewalls, which is the defining factor that separates them from other methods. One thing we can outrightly say here is that with this advantage, positive networks should be extended over to cloud environments, mobile devices, and endpoints. This allows you access to the identification and reduction of risk and threat vectors across your network environment, and from there, you can create the right protection system for yourself as well as your business while preserving a simple and effective security policy.

Looking at the working environment now, looking for a way to extend positive control over to all used applications irrespective of the port is not a simple task. This is the case because some of the applications used by employees connected to your network are meant for personal purposes. Social media platforms are multifunctional platforms that can be used for personal and official purposes, and this is where positive stretching control might get a little bit tricky.

This is, however, possible as organizations can make it a policy for departments in organisations not to use certain types of applications that do not have any correlation to the company while connected to the office network. This policy makes it paramount that only certain types of applications with certain approved features can function on the office network.

To reduce the level of attack on a network on endpoints and in virtual environments, the following must be done by organizations:

- Every network traffic must go through positive control to avoid cyberattacks even when port evasion techniques and encryptions are used to hide incoming traffic.

- Companies must make policies on the type of applications that are approved on the office network as well as the uses based on the needs at work simply by determining the following:

  A. The types of devices that are allowed to connect to the network as well as strict compliance policies that would ensure compliance.

B. What sort of data can be distributed across the IT and non-IT apps.

C. What sort of applications can be used on the network in the cloud as well as on the network.

D. The applications required for the activities of the day and who have access to make use of them.

E. What personal applications do you want to allow as an organisation.

Controlling applications that constitute advanced malware

The lifecycle of cyberattacks is heavily dependent on the use of applications as it is the major factor for initiating the infection as well as the continuous command in a bid to hit the target. From the perspective of security, emails and viruses work together, and even though the email method of attack is still used by attackers, it has lost some of the power it had back then as many organizations take email security very seriously. This has caused attackers to shift perspective from emails down to applications that relate with users in real-time, resulting in a more threatening opportunity for attackers. This move to the use of applications by attackers helps then hide under the umbrella of social interactions while hiding the presence of an imminent infiltration. These social and personal apps are the target applications for attackers as they have become the most common source of malware infection as well as contentious control from there on in.

Phishing attacks that make use of email applications are still in use by cybercriminals who try to deceive people on your network into revealing sensitive information or clicking malicious links. Many of these applications are made to pass information in a variety of ways, and this works because people make use of them with disguised thrust and a careless attitude simply because they are used to making use of the applications outside the office environment. Once this is done, there is a new window of opportunity for attackers to infect your network.

Many social applications are available today for personal as well as social engineering purposes. This dual-purpose makes it easy for a cybercriminal to pose as someone else, which lures you into clicking a link without suspecting anything. Even with all the sophistication that the malware has, it still cannot simply force its way through the application, but rather, it works by enticing an unsuspecting user to perform a misguided action such as the clicking of a malicious link. Instead of the usual email attachment, it might be the use of a link that moves you over to your Facebook page, enticing you to input your password to reveal your social media details, and once this is done, they are in your system already.

Also, with the use of security technology and tools comes the need for training staff on security awareness and also training end-users on security strategies that they need to remain safe and protect themselves against social engineering tactics.

Dynamically test files that are unknown

We know that malware and exploits are dynamic and easily modified by the cyber criminals, so the cyberattacks would not be noticed, triggering known signatures. The dynamic nature of the malicious technology which allows the attacker to enter into the network without drawing any suspicions by the security system.

For you to adjust to the dynamic nature of cyberattacks, you have to understand and be able to integrate new technology created based on the new threats and the behaviors that they have, not just based on the simple outlook. This dynamic analysis can be performed by the simple execution of files that are suspicious in an environment that can run and detect such files. This would help to see and understand what can be done by the threat, providing a way to detect new threats.

Still, detection is just one side of the puzzle, enforcing against factors that would cause these threats is something you have to take into consideration if the security and safety of your network and its users is your top priority. This means that the active examination of new malicious networks must constantly be linked with a next-generation firewall as well as cloud-based security solutions and advanced endpoint protection. Typically, in-line enforcement includes the following:

- Automated Instruments that can help you aid in remediation efforts.

- Defense from threats that make use of related URLs and domains

- Reports of communicative indicators of concession for which you can identify the infected parts of the network.

- Protection from threats that take advantage of the same control strategy and command.

- Dynamic protection for variants and unknown malware.

- Defense from newly identified malware infrastructure and command and control server. You can also control enabling applications by:

a. Checking out all risky traffic and applications and making sure that it is permitted, making use of trusted network design as well as segmentation that would improve the next-generation firewall providing full malware protection and URL filtering.

b. Selectively decrypting SSL traffic based on the URL and application category. An example of this is the decryption of the sites, which can be used as a point of entry, such as your webmail without accessing the financial traffic of the network as it is private.

c. Preventing the use of compromised web pages, which would, without notice, download malicious files.

d. Totally blocking the use of applications without purpose in terms of organizational use.

- Limiting the use of applications for users and groups that have genuine and accepted work needs.

- Disabling specific features, such as desktop sharing, tunneling, and file transfer.

The best practices in security dictates that applications and data that have something to do with the organization be kept and used in secure parts of the network based on the principles of zero thrust. Zero thrusts are upfront by making use of policies based on applications and user identity as well as firewalls. In cloud environments, direct communication in server hosts occur constantly, and in most cases across different levels of thrust, making subdivision a big problem. Having different levels of thrust when linked with a lack of traffic visibility by port-based security offerings might deteriorate your security.

Preventing the use of circumventors

Web-based applications and common end-user applications can be corrupted by malware for use against the company, which was targeted in the first place. It is equally important to note that other class of applications is designed to dodge the usual network security. Some of these applications include the following:

- Circumventing applications

- Remote desktop techs

- Proxies

Many of these applications are useful in the work environment while others do not, but in all cases, there is a need for control to stop unmanaged threat vectors into the company. Many of these remote desktop technologies are prevalent amongst IT support teams, and end-users, and many of them have the ability to control the endpoint of an end-user.

These technologies mentioned here have two risks:

- When a user connects to a remote PC, he has the capacity to move to any destination and connect to any applications without the traffic being intercepted by the installed firewall. In addition to the avoidance policy, there is an unmanaged threat vector that is opened by the remote desktop when a user goes through many risky behaviors, which lead to results that eventually affect the endpoint of the organization.

- The use of remote desktop technology allows users who are unsanctioned access inside the organisation's trust network. This sort of control is the objective of the malware, and this then creates an opportunity for cybercriminals to launch invasions that affect the company.

Many mutual applications that are usually used in organisations can also lead to unintended exposure if not used properly or if used by untrained or unauthorized users. Many of these applications have to be used by trained individuals or at least by individuals who have the approval for use with login monitoring and tight control.

Finally, many of the encrypted tunneling applications have been advanced to provide users with secure communication across established firewalls as well as other secure infrastructures. Many proxy technologies, such as the PHProxy, provide users with an easy way to move through the network securely without any organisational control whatsoever. These applications are some of the best security infrastructures and are updated regularly on the state of insecurity, so they remain undetected. Examples of these applications are UltraSurf and Tor, and these applications have no valid use in organisations, which means that once they are used, they are there as a means they avoid security. These application types are typically used in high-risk behaviors such as accessing sites that have blocked content, which, when accessed, carry high risks of malware infection. In most cases, these apps should not be allowed to function.

You can prevent the use of circumventors by doing the following:

- Restricting the use of remote desktop to specific personnel such as IT support.

- Allowing SSH but preventing SSH Tunneling.

- Instantly blocking encrypted tunnels and proxies which are unapproved such as Hamachi.

Taking out time to examine unknown traffic and unknown traffic patterns

As a company, business, or big organization, once you have regained positive control over your network and now have the ability to review and precisely classify the sort of traffic which is approved on the network, it can then classify what is left of the traffic on the entire network. For the sort of network which we are looking at here, which is the malware network, it is often recognized by the system firewall as unknown due to the use of proprietary encryption.

Now, compared to the usual firewall systems which allow traffic to pass based on protocols of approved ports, you have more with the new and advanced firewall systems. With the advanced firewall system, you can search the network and analyze the traffic where you can then determine whether or not the traffic is generated from a genuine source or not. With the advanced malware you as well as your security team, depending on the size of your organizations, have the capacity to know where the traffic is going under some criteria such as the following:

Is the transmission schedule regular?

✓   Does the content eventually go out to social media sites or even other malicious websites?

✓   Do you notice any user trying to upload or download a file to a URL that is unknown?

Once any of these mentioned situations happen to occur, then you know that malware is present on the client endpoint. With the use of the advanced firewall, you can accurately pinpoint traffic on the network there would hardly be a case of unknown traffic which somewhat used to be prevalent on the network, thus increasing the ease of finding and responding to malicious traffic on the network.

Gradually, these advanced next-generation firewalls do more than just helping with the analysis of the unknown traffic but also analyzes unknown files automatically, to identify malicious activities and threats to the network. With this, you have time to focus your search on the unknown traffic and files as well. This is so important because anything unknown on a network should be quickly examined, analyzed, and then handled. For you to systematically and quickly manage unknown traffic patterns, you have to do the following:

✓ Making use of behavioral malware reports as well as other reporting tools to understand and determine whether certain traffic is a threat or not.

✓ Making use of packet captures to record unknown traffic and then report it to your safety vendor.

✓ Applying firewall policies that help view and inspect unknown traffic or totally block it off.

✓ Preventing traffic to URLs that are malicious.

✓ Determining the internal apps which are on the network and create a custom signature or apply an override on the application.

✓ Analyzing unknown files to determine whether it is malicious or not.

✓ Monitoring the traffic to URLs that are unknown and blocking future uploads or downloads from that site.

Also, analyze and investigate any unknown traffic for malware activities and users who are unauthorized by doing the following:

✓ Delivering PCAPs to your security vendor for more analysis and a successful identification.

✓ Take time to track the source, the endpoint, and the volume of the unknown traffic.

✓ Define custom application IDs for any internal or custom application.

✓ Compare IPS, URL, malware, and file transfer records.

Getting infected hosts using advanced next-generation firewalls

Even when you get the best control systems up and running, it is inevitable that endpoints would get infected by malware through different means like their USB drives, unknown vectors, or new malware. The analysis of these threats might take a lot of time, and during the time of this analysis, before we get to know what it is, the malware has the capacity to infect even the most secure systems. It is, therefore, important for you to always assume that there is an infection on the endpoint, and at this point, you just need to develop the necessary patterns to finding these infections on the network. This task can be a difficult one since this malware has already evaded the usual malware signatures, which has given it root access on the endpoint, which is already infected.

For you to know the endpoint which is infected, you have to shift your focus from the usual things, which are malware signatures to the analysis of network behaviors that are unusual that are observed on the network. As we have said time and time again, for a network to function there must be communication, and the communication which is used by malware networks is most difficult to detect. At this point, you need to create patterns that can be used to identify the behavioral patterns of this malware, which are different from the usual network pattern even though it's a completely unknown malware pattern.

The combination of endpoint protection which prevents malware and exploits, combined with the advanced next-generation firewalls can provide an extra layer of context around the traffic going through your network and create a safe environment so that the rate of infection is less likely to occur even if malware wiggles its way through the network defenses.

The outcome derived from your analysis should include reports on information observed during the time of infection and execution, as well as other unique patterns delivered to security enforcement products. This capacity would help you detect the location of this malware on the endpoint, which is infected to prevent the spread of these threats in the future.

A simple example is the analysis of information on malicious domains and URLs. Here a threat feed can help determine malicious communication channels, and then your security team can locate the endpoints connected to them for any indicators of compromise.

Locate command and control traffic

Amongst the numerous benefits of the advanced firewall, one major advantage is the ability to classify the complicated and different traffic streams on the application level. This includes your ability to scan through the traffic progressively and then remove any protocols running within the protocols until the main application is identified. It is very important to be able to identify intricate traffic, as it is important for detecting the unique command and control communications of advanced cybercriminals. One important fact is that malware is an application, and it has unique traffic, which can be recognized only by making use of the new and advanced next-generation firewalls.

Automatically track and correlate

In previous sections, we analyzed different techniques that are useful, but the time and the resources are not available most of the time. From the installation of advanced firewall systems over to the advanced endpoint protection as well as other intelligence systems that come together for full protection of the systems. For example, the new advanced next-generation firewalls can provide you with information about the following:

(a) **IRC Traffic (Internet Relay Chat):** this is a common and well-known communication method used by malware, and when you find this, you have full confidence that there is a malware infection.

(b) **Unknown UDP (User Datagram Protocol)/TCP (Transmission Control Protocol):** The APT traffic is usually unknown and encrypted, so, the best thing to do would be to start tracking UDP and TCP traffic in a bid to find endpoints that are infected.

(c) **Making use of IP addresses rather than domain names:** many of the new and advanced malware makes use of IP addresses compared to the usual browsing, which makes use of URK addresses, and this is worth noting.

(d) **Newly registered domains:** for moving around as well as recovery, malware always makes use of newly registered domains. It is not a conclusive fact, but it is highlighted that visits to newly registered websites can be a sign of infection.

(e) **Dynamic DNS (Domain Name System):** the dynamic DNS is used by malware for moving from one infected host to the other with many new IP addresses making it hard to track the destination as well as the source of malware.

(f) **Recognized malware sites:** the use of the URL filtering engine of the advanced firewall consistently tracks sites with hosted malware, whether intentionally or unintentionally.

With the identification of these indicators, it is important to act on them quickly. This is achievable through open APIs, native integration, and technical partnerships that feed the combined information for a solution. The automated process can then quarantine the endpoint, which is affected and then take more action as it is needed.

Chapter 5

Making Advanced Threat Policies for Protection

Most of the time, many technical solutions are employed without considering the implication of implementing this on the business and their organisation's overall security strategies. To prevent this from being the case, your policies have to be up to date with technological solutions that you want to use and should be comprehensive enough as well.

In this chapter, we are going to be considering different types of controls we must take into consideration if an organization would need to boast of working security policies. Let's go.

Safe enablement via smart policies

The main reason why we take security policies seriously is so we can prevent our networks from being infected by these advanced threats rather than other methods of locating and removing infections afterward. However, even with these security policies, most networks are susceptible to attacks. With this in mind, even with these policies, you need to assume the worst and tell yourself that at some point, your network is going to be attacked.

The security policies you create for your organization must help in the fight against malware and reduce infection risks, which comes from the use of different applications and features on your network for business and user requirements.

If you have an IT department, then they have an important role to play in defining smart policies that help the company, as well as the users, reduce the risk, which is attached to the use of various applications and features on the network. Irrespective of their usefulness towards the formulation of the best security policies, it should not be done by the IT department alone as the input of the executives is also important in making sure that the policies are functional and again usable.

The use and adoption of these security policies start from the users and once this is fully integrated into the operational part of the company, the removal or creation of new policies for these users can be extremely difficult even if management says they have a hand in it – therefore, the creation of these policies should be done when every aspect of the organizations functionality has been taken into consideration.

Looking at an environment that needs security and is well regulated, we take a peek at the stock market. In this market, the use of features like instant messaging would be subject to auditability and retention rules. The IT team in the organization helps educate users and traders on the risks connected with the use of instant messaging apps and then monitor and enforce the use of these tools an example of this is preventing traders from using messaging apps like Facebook messenger while trading but then enable the use of internal chat servers instead.

Application Controls

The art of knowing and understanding network users, the behavior they have when using the network, their applications, and associated risks. For certain applications needed to function at work but not controlled by the IT department, these are the major points of risk and obvious threats. It is, therefore, important to match the needs of users with the right type of applications while enlightening them on the risks attached to the use of these applications and features.

Allowing or enabling the use of certain applications includes the restriction of useless and high-risk applications while supervising the allowed applications to prevent the risks attached to the use. Establishing effective policies requires discussions amongst users, IT, and management, so together; there can be an understanding of applications that have legitimate value when it comes to working. There are many applications out there today known to be the nests of malware attacks both for infection and continuous command and control. One of the most applications in this category is BitTorrent.

Also, many applications are not in the category of good applications; neither are they termed as bad, which means that these sorts of applications would be located in the gray area of the company's security policy. This is because these applications might be useful for the organization but still pose a potential risk for the company. The objective of this sort of application is safe enablement. Here the applications can be allowed but constrained to allow only the features that are needed while blocking unwanted and risky features. An example is a company allowing web meeting applications but blocking the high-risk features like remote desktop capabilities which can give a cybercriminal remote access to the system. Using policies would also limit certain applications and features to certain approved users, and the application could be scanned to make sure that no unapproved file or content is moved through the system. The main objective is to limit the risk in the use of the application rather than limiting the application itself.

The use of application controls should be part of the organizational security policy of organizations. IT should make increased efforts to learn about the evolving world of web-based applications in a bid to implement application control policies. Doing this means acceptance of these apps for all of their intended purposes, and if it is necessary, there should be a sort of proactive installation or enablement in the lab environment to see the behavior.

Strict User Controls

Another method is strict user control, which many companies make use of. Here, this means that for every application, there would be usage policies outlining which applications can be used and those that cannot be used. With this everyone working in the company is expected to understand the application usage content, the policies as well as the consequences of not complying, but some questions still remain unanswered from our survey of companies in this position of strict user control:

✓ With the increasing number of applications being developed daily, how can staff have an understanding of the apps which are allowed, and the ones that are not allowed?

✓ How is the list of apps which are not approved updated, and who is in charge of letting employees know that the list has been updated?

✓ What can we actually define as a policy violation?

✓ What are the consequences of policy violations – termination or warnings?

It is often a big task to develop policy guidelines as many of the factors which constitute these policies often clash, leading to policy creation problems. Having to find out what is to be allowed as well as what should be prohibited is a daunting task because this has to be done through the horoscope of security and safety and the opinion of major stakeholders in the company.

Another factor that makes this more of a daunting task is that the new applications and web-based applications are not within the control of those in the IT department and are often adopted by users most of the time before appropriate policies concerning use are put into consideration and developed.

The key factors that need to be employed by organizations as part of application control are the training of end-users as well as the documentation of employee policies and not one without the other because then it is insufficient for safe enablement of the new and ever-changing applications. Look at it this way; if you need to prevent your users from uploading sensitive information, you need to train users and lay policies for employees rather than leaving the matter to employee faith and user discretion – this is not a movie.

Network Controls

Since the network is the foundation of attacks for advanced threats and the ongoing command and control afterward, there is a need for critical policy enforcements. Segmenting networks is a necessity with firewalls at the boundaries of different data divisions, to make sure that data is inspected as it moves through the different segments of the network. With the policies selecting which applications can and cannot be used, the IT department of a company can then go on to inspecting the content which has been allowed through the network.

Talking about this inspection, it is all about moving through the network and scanning for malware dangerous URLs, exploits, control patterns, and finally, the continuous command and control. If it is possible, policies that are made to go through the content of traffic should be organized as a single policy where all the rules can be identified. If these rules cover multiple solutions, putting together a logical policy for enforcement becomes gradually difficult for security staff and your IT team no matter how good they are. To make matters worse, the knowledge of whether these policies are working would also be difficult for the IT team, which is very worrisome, I must say.

The ideal objective would be to make written policies that reflect the intention of the policy just as if it is being described. For example, only a few sets of employees are allowed to make use of certain apps; inspect all the app traffic for malware; do not allow the transfer of certain file types, and scan for confidential traffic going to network locations that are untrusted.

Putting things this way is important for preventing malware infection from moving through the system, infecting all that comes its way. If you have proper policy anytime malware tries to move through the network; it would eventually be detected and stopped due to the policy violation attempted by the malware as well as access restrictions.

Another important part of the network policies is the total need to retain the visibility of the content in the traffic. A commonly used secure traffic destination on the internet is the SSL. Even though this may provide secure traffic for a short period, if an IT team does not have the capacity to go through the SSL tunnel, the SSL would then make an invisible path for the malware to go through into the network environment. The company's IT team must balance the need to look into SSL against the overall performance requirements of the network as well as the privacy requirement for users. So, it is important to begin SSL decryption policies, for SSL which can be selectively enforced URL category and user groups

Controlling Endpoints

Most of the time, the first-choice target for advanced malware cybercriminals is the end-user computer, and this is a point which requires huge policy enforcements, users at endpoints should find a way to make sure that majority of the host-based security solutions like antiviruses are installed in their devices and updated as at when due. Also, there is need to make sure that the operating system of hosts is up to date, and this is because the majority of malware infections start with exploiting remote vulnerabilities, which targets a hole in the application or overall, the operating system.

This is why it is important to make sure that all systems are up to date if fending off malware attacks is ever going to be possible. This is, however, easier said than done when talking about maintaining and updating system updates. Just like employee policies, desktop control is an important part of keeping applications safe in organizations. The problem with desktop control is that it is a bit challenging even for IT personnel's and when done, there is need for careful consideration as it has an impact on the productivity of employees this is because once desktop control is established, the system is practically on lockdown, preventing employees from installing apps of their own and for a lot of reasons it's much harder than you think and if this is the only implemented plan, it would definitely not work for the following reasons:

✓   There are many applications put there today capable of running on USB, which means that a web-based application can run once there is access to the network.

✓   For PC's that are remotely connected, internet downloads and emails are possible ways of getting applications that are not allowed into the system and on the network.

✓   Removing all administrative rights is difficult to implement mainly because it has huge effects on what the end-user can and cannot do to a level that hampers progress.

Many of the endpoint protection products which are available right now are usually facing one side of the problem, mostly the detection and removal of viruses. This is a technique that has been continuously used for many years with little or nothing to show for it.

For some of the new security protocols out there, we have the incorporation of new protocols like cloud-based signature updates, anti-malware, host-based intrusion prevention, and personal firewalls, but even with all of these put together, it is no match for new and advanced malware out there today.

End-point controls are signature less, help's with these situations, and when malware or exploits try to get to the endpoint, these controls get to identify specific properties of malware and then prevent them from having their way in the system and eventually in the network. The endpoint protection, which is more advanced, requires a complete approach that integrates other solutions for full security. There is a different mindset required for advanced endpoint protection compared to traditional methods. Therefore, since the advanced malware is the way forward, the following must be implemented:

✓ Closely integrated with network and cloud security for fast data exchange and organizational protection.

✓ Prevent every exploit.

✓ Prevent every malware without knowledge of all malware signatures.

✓ Be scalable so as to integrate into all applications without any disruptions.

A point for mobile and remote users

Many of our new and advanced companies are more than they used to be, just as the technology has improved as well. With technological advancements, many of the users simply expect to connect to work from anywhere in the world, whether at home, the airport, and even on the subway. This has been a trend for organizations with many organizations implementing 'bring your own device' and 'bring your own app' policies. This implementation means that the data of many workers in the organization might be beyond reach and far from the protection of the security perimeter solutions available.

Where is the solution here? The only way to go about this is to build a security plan which does not take these mobile devices as a different part of the company. They require the same application and content protection even when they are outside the protection they would receive if they were still within the perimeter. Building consistent security architecture requires a lot of planning, and this planning and implementation is a must for any company wishing to address the complexity in modern computing.

Also, many of the security policies implemented must address the use of endpoint devices other than the standard organizational equipment. Many of the computer users who work from home or at least anywhere away from the company make use of their PCs, which is likely to be running on Windows or Apple as well as other devices such as iOS, Android, and tablets all connected to the network. These devices have to be taken into consideration to prevent holes in the security of your organization.

You have to note that over the years, mobile malware has increasingly become a problem as many people prefer to use them over their PCs with a lot of personal and organizational data kept unsafe and unprotected.

Chapter 6

Cyber security: The Solution

As we have browsed through the entire hemisphere on cyberattacks and cybersecurity, we are going to be looking into considerations that you have to look at so you can evaluate which of the cybersecurity protocols fits your present condition and your organizational objectives. This has to be a personal decision based on your company as well as what benefits your standards.

Enforce allowed data connection between users and your data

For you to reduce the number of attacks that your data and your overall network face, you need to have a cyber-solution that would help you identify all the interactions between your users and your network, and this is mostly for the data you are trying to protect. This means you have to make use of a solution which allows for micro-segmentation. This is because every network behaves differently, and with the difference in each of these networks comes the need for different types of behaviors allowed. So, at this junction, the identification of the different levels of users according to their level of privilege and the kind of data they need to have access to. The policies which you make must be enforced within the application navigating the network and the transactions that are expected of them. The use of gritty network policies is the best way to reduce the surface of attack blocking unauthorized services in the process of providing the fundamentals of outgoing and incoming traffic.

Identify Threats Everywhere

Data is always moving from physical to virtual locations via the use of different ports, protocols, and applications. The lateral movement of machine-to-machine communication symbolizes movements, but these movements are ones that are hardly monitored, which is a big opportunity for a cybercriminal. There is data all over the place moving within instruments like the ATM, wireless cameras, printers, and POS machines, all of which are used by attackers to move beyond the traditional firewall and security systems in many organizations.

The solution to this is a thorough end-to-end identification of all apps, devices, and users in all locations on or within the network of the organization if cybersecurity is ever going to be a possibility.

Protect data in different stages of the attack lifecycle

Security tools that are standalone like web proxies only focus on one stage of the attack, and this is bound to fail specifically because of the new and advanced techniques which are used by attackers. A good and effective strategy for preventing this is the use of coordinated technologies which detect and prevent these attacks at different stages of infection, and this would help to block all the known as well as unknown threats which mean we would be able to stop attackers from attaining their goals and objectives.

You have to select cybersecurity solutions which focus on the behavior of these attacks at the different stages by this we mean:

- Limiting movement through segmentation.
- Protecting against exploit kits as well as application vulnerabilities.

- Blocking delivery through malicious files and compromised web pages.
- Stopping all outboard command-and-control communication.
- Stopping file execution, which contains known malware through payload identification.

The ability to reduce the surface of attack alongside full visibility and prevention mechanisms at all stages means that as the attack moves on, there is a slightly lower chance that it would succeed, which means that the chances of a secure network would always increase per time.

Outwit the threats designed to outsmart security tools

The tools in cybersecurity which have the capacity to protect in the form of static signatures that are unique and broad are inadequate since they can only protect against known threats such as:

- Communication via a popular command-and-control center.
- A known malware delivered from a known malicious URL.

Many of the attackers have become wiser and have taken time to edit and modify the exploits of their malware, making them unknown and then able to move past the defenses of the system. The changes made on these networks make it difficult for security systems to keep safe more so, these malware and command-and-control centers come and go for most of the time, leaving the system and entering whenever as a different system entirely.

The number of exploits and malware available today makes it compulsory that security systems that can handle these variations be made, and this is either by having a big and growing library of hash-based signatures and exploits which are capable of detecting and then preventing many variations as they come. Smart signatures which are capable of identifying threats inside every file, and every protocol, exploit, file types, and hashes help increase the level of security as well as the same level of protection against new and sometimes reused attack components.

Translate new information into protections in security policies

Looking at more than half of the number of attacks, it happens within minutes. With the speed of infections, there is a need for quick translation of data into intelligence and then into enforced security measures, allowing the prevention of the infection of network and device infection in real-time and less reliance on manual remedies.

You have to make sure that your systems are up to date, preventing openings in prevention processes and capabilities such as URL hosting exploits, new malware payloads, and command-and-control server positions into protection, which can be enforced by the usual technologies used on the networks.

This process can work better when it is self-automated, allowing a newly created feed of newly created protection against new attacks filed down to smaller parts making for better protection moved over to the points for protection within different parts of the network, this allows for a more effective cybersecurity solution.

Get information and protection against up-to-date attacks

The threat environment is constantly changing as the attackers are changing their methods of attacks, and they are trying as much as possible to become less obvious than they were before. These attackers understand the changing hemisphere of the world of technology today and are doing all they can to become less obvious than they usually are. Knowing most of the preventive technologies and having security technologies that can handle them minimizes infections and stops cyber-attacks on its tracks. Even if this increases the cost of security, it helps to limit the number of attacks you have to deal with as a whole.

The world of cyberattacks is getting automated with numerous threats from every side, so your protection process needs to be automated as well to stay ahead of the developing and changing attack environment.

Allowing accurate and fast mitigation

Once you have faced a cyberattack that is sophisticated, the best line of defense is to perfect other devices as well as other important segments of the network to prevent further infection. This happens mostly because most defenses compromise of tools from different vendors, which makes preventive measures almost impossible. This is a highly manual, complicated, and time-consuming method mostly when threats are in different systems that are stored in different locations.

Getting infected does not mean that you have been breached because if you can find a way to stop the command-and-control communication, then you have effectively tackled the problem. This is not all you need to do as you need to find the affected system and then remove all infections. In addition to improving the capacity to prevent infections, technologies that take in a constant feed of threat information can help, and this is important because every second wasted is a time where attackers are doing more damage.

Consider a simple solution that matches behaviors that are suspicious to accurate alerts of infections, this way, you know that there is an infection coming up, and then you prioritize your systems accordingly, to limit infections. Many of the cybercriminals would try to take advantage of attack vectors, so it is important that the threat analysis tools cover all the parts of the device as well as the locations within the organization.

Organize actions across separate security technologies

Individual sensors and the overall security technologies contain a lot of info-gathering and enforcement capacities, if they are designed to work well together, have the capacity to make your dive towards making the organization more secure a huge success. Having the ability to identify the things happening at a certain stage of an attack and then link it to the bigger picture.

Once you are able to identify what is happening at every stage of an attack and then link it to the bigger picture of the attack you are on the best track to put a stop an imminent attack. This way, once you understand the objective of the attacker, you would know the point of entry as well as the steps to take to cover that gap immediately.

Keep your organization running

There are many organizations that find it difficult to make a good choice between securing the organization and allowing the numerous applications which improve employee productivity. Putting on security protection often means that users must follow the set rules or be restricted from using certain applications or even getting the data they need. Making the surface of attack smaller is important for maintaining usability. Also, the removal of unnecessary data interactions reduces the amount of traffic that would be scanned for threats, which reduces the amount of work your cyber tools would take on.

Since the task of continuity is very intensive, your security should be able to provide specific information for managing content, so traffic is processed only once.

Make things easy

Integrating data manually from different products can be somewhat a difficult task, which most of the time does not yield the right results. As time goes by after a compromise, the infection continues to spread, and the likelihood of your system being attacked with the eventual loss of information as a result is very high. This is not something that you can afford.

Therefore, you have to look for a cybersecurity vendor that makes use of security data both at the lower and higher global level, giving you access to actionable intelligence as well as threat campaigns.

Appendix

Adware: Pop-up marketing applications that typically have Freeware and Shareware installed.

Advanced persistent threat (APT): A Web-borne attack normally carried out by a wide number of individuals, such as organized crime and the rogue national state, with substantial wealth.

BitTorrent: P2P communication file-sharing protocol which distributes large quantities of data without having to incur the cost of hardware, host and bandwidth resources from the original distributor.

Backdoor: Malware that can circumvent standard authentication and obtain entry to a compromised device through an intruder.

Bootkit: A rootkit kernel-mode version widely used to connect complete disk protected computers.

Box: A SaaS-based, SSL secured cloud storage program. Corporate companies also use it so that people can freely and privately access, save and exchange data.

Botnet: A large and interactive network of bots.

Bot: A malware corrupted target computer that is part of a botnet.

Distributed denial-of-service (DDoS): A major attack, usually requiring the use of bots in a botnet to disrupt a specified server or network.

Dynamic DNS (DDNS): A method used to monitor in actual-time connected system domain name (DNS) information.

Drive-by download: Program, sometimes malware, is downloaded without user awareness or consent on a device from the internet.

Internet relay chat (IRC): A protocol of application layer that enables almost real-time contact within a customer-server network model.

IPsec: A software available to the public use and the IP for safe VPN communications.

Logic bomb: A collection of guidelines deliberately inserted in a system and the procedures are typically carried out with adverse consequences until a certain requirement is reached.

Master boot record (MBR): The first section of a computing unit includes details that indicate how and when an operating system is stored to load into the memory.

Malware: Malicious program or code, usually damaging or disabling, controlling or stealing computer device knowledge. It is usually composed of malware, Trojan horses, rootkits, and bootkits.

Nmap: A protection scanner used to identify hosts and resources for the network.

Next-generation firewall (NGFW): A port-based firewall that enforces device, consumer and client policies independent of port or protocol outside standard port-based controls.

Packet capture (PCAP): A Network Packet Collection API.

Remote Desktop Protocol (RDP): A patented Microsoft application allowing remote device control.

Rootkit: Malware of (root-level) unauthorized device access.

Skype: An internet service delivering instant updates, audio and video calls through the usage of contact technologies Audio over IP (VoIP).

Secure Sockets Layer (SSL): A transportation layer protocol which enables a safe connection between users and servers, based on session encryption and synchronization.

Secure Shell (SSH): A collection of protocols and a web protocol that offers a protected connection for a remote device.

Simple Mail Transfer Protocol (SMTP): An internet protocol that uses TCP port 25 for email transmission.

Spear phishing: A focused phishing campaign that appears to its targets more believable and therefore more likely to succeed. An entity or person that the receiver knows personally may be fooled by a spear-phishing text.

Trojan horse: A software to breach the protection of a computer device when executing an apparently harmless task.

Transmission Control Protocol (TCP): Connection-oriented protocol to link two hosts and to ensure the transmission in appropriate order of data and packets.

User Datagram Protocol (UDP): A protocol without link sometimes used in low-latency, time-sensitive interactions not needed to have guaranteed protocols.

Web widget: A tiny program which can be enabled and run by an end user on a web page.

FAQs

What are firewalls, and why are they used?

A firewall is a system monitoring mechanism in the network that tracks and manages traffic on device/network boundaries. Firewalls are used mainly to secure the network/system from viruses, worms, malware, etc. Internet exposure and web inspection may often be stopped through firewalls.

How does Hashing vary from Encryption?

Encryption and hashing are also used to transform recognizable data into a file that is unreadable. The downside is that during the decryption process, the authenticated data may be translated into actual data but not to the original information.

What is a three-way handshake?

- A three-way handshake is a way to establish a link between a server and a client in a TCP / IP network. It is regarded as a three-way handshake since the client and server share parquets in a three-step process. The following are three steps:

- If open ports are available, the server sends SYN-ACK packets to the client

- The client must send a SYN packet to the server to check that the server stands or has available ports.

- The client knows this and sends back the server with an ACK(Confirmation) packet.

What are the web application response codes that can be collected?

1xx .... Informational responses

2xx .... Success

3xx .... Redirection

4xx .... Client-side error

5xx .... Server-side error

What is traceroute? Why is it used?

Traceroute is a device showing a packet's direction. This lists all the places the packet crosses (mainly routers). This is primarily used when the package does not hit its target. To find the point of failure, it is used to validate when the link ends or falls.

Where can I have a firewall installed?

The steps to create a firewall are below:

- Username / Password: update the firewall system default password.

- Remote management: Disable the remote management feature.

- Port forwarding: Set up appropriate port forwarding that fits well for other programs such as an FTP server or site server.

- DHCP Server: Adding a firewall on a network with a current DHCP server can cause confusion unless the DHCP firewall is deactivated

- Logging: In order to fix issues with the Firewall due to future threats, ensure that logging is activated and recognize how to interpret logs.

- Policies: You will introduce strict protection policies to ensure that the firewall is designed to follow such policies.

Explain SQL Injection and how to prevent it?

Injection SQL Injection (SQLi) is an infection function where an intruder misleads a server's data with fraudulent SQL claims, thus accessing, altering, and removing unauthorized data to manage a web application's user database. This assault is used mainly to manipulate database servers.

Through the following methods, you can block SQL Injection attacks:

- Use Stored Procedures
- Use prepared statements
- Validate user input

What is a Brute Force Attack, and how can you prevent it?

Brute Force is a way of constantly attempting all the permutations and variations of available credentials to locate the correct credentials. In certain instances, brute force attempts are successful because the tool/software wants to sign in immediately for a permission list. There are various approaches to avoid assaults by the Brute Power. These are as follows:

The complexity of the password: using various character types in the password renders it more challenging through brute force assaults. Alpha-numeric codes and unique characters and top and bottom features boost the difficulty of the password, rendering it impossible to break.

Attempts Limiting Login: set a password failure limit, for example, the login failures limit can be raised to 3. Therefore, if you have three successive login faults, restrict the consumer to log in for a while or submit the next time, an email, or OTP to login. Since brute strength is an automatic operation, the brute force mechanism is interrupted by minimal login attempts.

Login Length: A minimum login duration may be built. The longer the secret, the more complicated it is to locate.

What is Port Scanning?

Port Scanning is the methodology for finding accessible ports and host facilities. Hackers are searching for details with port scanning, which can help hack weaknesses. Port Scanning is used by managers to track network protection policies. Several of the popular strategies for port scanning are:

- TCP Half-Open
- TCP Connect
- Ping Scan
- UDP
- Stealth Scanning

What is a VPN?

The virtual private network VPN is used for creating a safe and authenticated link. By utilizing a VPN, user information is transmitted to a point in the Network where it is authenticated and only distributed across the internet. Data should be decrypted and submitted to the server at this stage. When the server sends out a message, the response will be sent to an encoded point in the VPN, which will be sent to a new point in the VPN when the encoded data is decrypted. Finally, the consumer should obtain decrypted results. It is necessary to use the VPN to ensure the transmission of encrypted data.

Explain the MITM attack and how to prevent it?

A MITM attack is a kind of assault where the intruder puts themselves in two parties ' correspondence and robs the details. The assault is a MITM attack. Assume there is a correspondence between two entities A or B. This contact is then followed by the intruder. He shares Group B with A and Group A with B having A with him. All groups send the data to the hacker and, once the data is stolen, the hacker passes the data to the recipient party. Although all sides think they interact, they secretly communicate with the intruder.

Through the following strategies, you will avoid MITM attack:

- Use Intrusion Detection Systems
- Use VPN
- Force HTTPS
- Public Key Pair Based Authentication
- Use strong WEP/WPA encryption

Explain the DDOS attack and how to prevent it?

DDOS (Distributed Server denial) is a cyber-assault that makes servers fail to provide services to actual customers. There are two forms of DDOS attack:

Flooding attacks: the intruder sends a large amount of traffic to the server, which the server is unable to manage. Then the machine starts running. The assault is typically achieved by automatic processes, which submit packets to the server on an ongoing basis.

Crash attacks: criminals use a software error to crash a device, and the computer is then not able to supply the clients with services.

You can prevent DDOS attacks by using the following practices:

- Use Load Balancing
- Configure Firewalls and Routers
- Use Front-End Hardware
- Handle Spikes in Traffic
- Use Anti-DDOS services

What is an ARP, and how does it work?

ARP (Address Resolution Protocol) is a mechanism to chart a specific computer address known in the home network of the Internet Protocol Address.

If no IP address input is detected, ARP must send a message report to all of the devices on the LAN in a specific layout to see whether one computer understands it is an IP address.

The Gateway tells the ARP system to identify a logical host or MAC address representing the IP address if an incoming packet intended for an individual computer on a different local area network is reached.

In an ARP archive, the ARP system will search and, if it is able to locate the message, will supply the packet to be translated and sent to the computer to the proper packet duration and size.

What is a Botnet?

A Botnet is a collection of internet-linked computers with one or more bots operating on each machine—the bots on the computers that exploit a target and the harmful files. Botnets are used for stealing records, sending malware, and performing a DDOS attack.

Explain SSL and TLS

SSL is intended to test the identification of the source, but it will not try any further. SSL can allow you to identify individuals for whom you communicate, but it may also often be fooled.

TLS is also a method for detecting SSL, but it provides better protection. It provides enhanced data security and also incorporates SSL and TLS to enhance privacy.

Explain Phishing and how to prevent it?

Phishing is a malware assault where the intruder camouflages himself as a familiar individual or company and tries using fake e-mails or instant messages to capture confidential monetary or personal details.

By utilizing the following methods, you will avoid phishing attacks:

- Do not insert any personal details into the sites you have no confidence
- Using anti-virus tools
- Use Online safety Toolbar
- Check the Protection of the web site
- Using firewalls

What is the difference between IDS and IPS?

IDS is the intrusion detection device that recognizes cyberattacks only, and the admin needs to ensure the attack is prevented. In IPS, the device senses infiltration and often takes steps to avoid invasion. The program often identifies interference in the network.

What is Cryptography?

Cryptography is the science and research of information-security and interaction methods, primarily directed at preserving third-party data for which this code serves no function.

Explain CIA triad

Confidentiality, integrity, and accessibility are what the CIA portrays. CIA is a blueprint to direct cyber management strategies. It's one of the organization's most famous ones.

Confidentiality

Only approved workers must be able to view and interpret the content. Unauthorized workers will not be accessible. The database can be heavily secured even when anyone uses malware to access the data, so it is not legible or recognizable, even though the data is obtained.

Integrity

Ensuring that no unauthorized party has changed the details. Integrity ensures that non-staff do not manipulate or change the records. When an authorized person/system attempts to alter the data and the modification has failed, the data will be corrected and not manipulated.

Availability

Once the user asks, the details will be accessible to the customer. Software repairs, frequent updates, data transfers, and recovery, service gaps will be accounted for.

What is the difference between Vulnerability Assessment and Penetration Testing?

Vulnerability Assessment is a method to recognize the victim's shortcomings. Here, the company understands that the machine/service has faults or vulnerabilities, so they want to recognize such faults and eliminate defects.

Penetration testing is the method of defining the destination's weaknesses. If so, the company will have defined what compliance mechanisms it would recommend and would prefer to check whether the machine/service would otherwise be compromised.

Explain SSL Encryption

The proprietary encryption infrastructure SSL (Secure Sockets Layer) builds authenticated communications between a Server and a Client. It is used for data security and electronic purchases to safeguard details. The following measures are needed to create an SSL connection:

- A client attempts to link to a protected SSL site server
- A copy of the SSL certificate is sent from your computer to the server
- The client verifies whether or not the SSL certificate is valid. If safe, the user sends a response to the site server asking for an authenticated path.
- The database server gives a message to initiate an encrypted SSL link.
- SSL secures that correspondence between the client and the site server takes place

What is the difference between HIDS and NIDS?

HIDS (Host IDS) and NIDS (Network IDS) also help to identify cyberattacks and operate for the same reason. The only variation being the HIDS setup is on a different server. It tracks traffic and irregular network behaviors of a specific unit. NIDS is built on a server on the other side. This traffic tracks all network tools.

What is Cognitive Cybersecurity?

The implementation of AI strategies modeled on human behavior mechanisms to identify risks and defend physical and digital networks is cognitive cybersecurity.

Self-learning protection mechanisms mimic the human mind through data analysis, pattern detection, and interpretation of the natural language, also in a high-power machine model.

What steps will you take to secure a server?

For data encryption and decryption, stable servers use the Stable Sockets Layer (SSL) protocol to defend data against illegal interception.

Four easy ways to protect server are available:

Phase 1: Make sure the root and server users have a safe login.

Phase 2: Allow new users to your network and then install the firewall rules in remote access utilizing root users to control the device.

Phase 3: Remote Access from the normal kernel/administration accounts.

Phase 4: The next phase is to configure the network access firewall guidelines.

What is 2FA, and how can it be implemented for public websites?

The external protection mechanism dubbed "multi-factor authentication."

Not only includes a login and username but anything that only the user has, i.e., just details they would learn or have to manage–like a tangible key.

Authenticator programs remove the need for fax, voice call, or emails to obtain an authentication token.

What are salted hashes?

Salt is a spontaneous bit of information. If you use a fresh password from a correctly secured password scheme, a random salt value is generated, and a composite value is saved in its database. This helps shield you from dictionary attacks and established hash attacks.

Example: When someone uses the same password on two separate systems and uses the same hashing algorithm, the hash value will be identical, but the meaning will be separate only that one program uses the hashes with salt.

What is data leakage?

Data Leakage is a deliberate or accidental leakage of data from a business to an unintentionally unknown location. It is the release of an unauthorized party of classified knowledge. In 3 types, a data leak can be broken down depending on how it occurs:

Unintentional breach: an agency transfers data accidentally to an illegitimate individual because of a mistake or error.

Deliberate violation: the approved entity would intentionally submit data to an illegal entity.

Device Hack: Data leakage is achieved through hacking strategies.

The usage of resources, applications, and techniques named DLP (Data Leakage Prevention) will prevent data leaks.

What is port blocking within LAN?

Port blocking is also restricting users ' right to access a range of networks inside the local area network.

To avoid the source from utilizing ports and not reach the target node, as the code runs on the ports, they are disrupted to limit access to the networks filling of safety holes.

What are the different layers of the OSI model?

An OSI is a standard model to connect programs through a service. The aim of an OSI guide is to direct providers and programmers to communicate with code and wireless communication goods.

Physical Layer: Digital data transfer through communications media from sender to recipient.

Data Link Layer: performs data transfer to and from a terminal server. It can encrypt and decrypt data bits too.

Network Layer: Accountable for packet transfer and network traffic routing.

Transport layer: accountable for end-to-end network connectivity. It separates data from the upper layer and transmits it to the network layer and guarantees that the whole data has hit the recipient's end safely.

Session Layer: Controls sender-receiver link. The session is started, terminated, and controlled, and the relationship amongst the sender and recipient is created, retained, and Synchronized.

Presentation layer: It tackles displaying the data in an appropriate format and information layout rather than submitting raw packets or datagrams.

Application Layer: offers a network-to-device gateway. This emphasizes on coordination between the systems and offers a collaboration interface.

What are black hat, white hat, and gray hat hackers?

Gray hat hackers are a combination of black hat hackers with a white hat. Without approval from the creator, they are searching for device weaknesses. They send it to the owner if they notice any weaknesses. They will not take advantage of the bugs, unlike Black hat hackers.

Black hat hackers are renowned for their deep understanding of computer networking. The malware that can be used for accessing such networks can be released. The hackers abuse their power to access information or to maliciously exploit the compromised device.

White hat hackers use their skills effectively and are often referred to as Conscientious Hackers. They are primarily hired by businesses to find bugs and protection problems in applications as a technology professional. They use their ability to enhance security.

What do you understand by Risk, Vulnerability & Threat in a network?

- Threat: Somebody that may damage a device or a corporation.
- Vulnerability: Weakness in a device that a possible intruder might manipulate.
- Risk: Loss or harm opportunity when the hazard leverages a weakness.

How can identity theft be prevented?

This is what you should do to stop the abuse of identity:

- Shop on well-known websites.

- Use the most current client update.

- Provide an efficient and special password.

- Install sophisticated malware and software for spyware.

- Using advanced financial data management tools.

- Update the device and applications often.

- Secure your social security number (SSN).

- Do not exchange confidential information publicly, notably on social platforms.

How would you reset a password-protected BIOS configuration?

BIOS is a pre-boot device, and it has its own configuration and priorities management process. One easy way to re-establish the CMOS battery is to kill its power source by saving the memory and losing its layout as a result.

How often should you perform Patch management?

As soon as it is released, patch management will be completed. For windows, it must be extended to all computers no later than one month after the patch is published. The same applies to network equipment, as soon as it is published, to fix it. Reasonable patch management is required.

Explain the XSS attack and how to prevent it?

XSS (Cross-Site Scripting) is a cyber-attack which permits hackers into the Webpage to insert malicious customer-side scripts. You can use XSS for hijacking sessions and the stealing of cookies, changing DOM, executing remote codes, crashing the site, etc.

These attacks can be prevented by:

- Encode special characters
- Use XSS HTML Filter
- Validate user inputs
- Sanitize user inputs
- Use Anti-XSS services/tools

SQL Programming

Learn the Ultimate Coding,

Basic Rules of the Structured

Query Language for Databases

like Microsoft SQL Server (Step-

By-Step Computer

Programming for Beginners)

Table of Contents

Introduction

In this book, SQL Programming, you will be introduced to the world of programming and guided through all of the important features one needs to be familiar with as a beginner.

When it comes to SQL programming, there is quite a lot to learn so as to apply it to a career or a hobby.

Regardless, rest assured that the content within these chapters will provide you with the necessary information needed for clear understanding of it all.

First, this book will give you a clear comprehension of what SQL programming is with a short historical background, SQL query types, database advantages and disadvantages.

Followed by a discussion about the administration of the database and how to attach and detach databases.

Finally, a close look at how to create some of the necessary tables, the different tools that are required to get the work done, and so much more.

If you are using a database to learn more about your customers, figure out best-selling products, or other SQL related processes this guide book will come in handy.

For beginners, this guide book simplifies the SQL language and its benefits.

Chapter 1:

Introduction to SQL

SQL (Structured Query Language) is a programming language that has become standardized in the designation of data management and storage. Because of this, a person with a little know-how can easily manipulate, parse, and create any type of data.

Throughout the years, we've witnessed the hype of many modern tech businesses shifting their business towards data-driven strategies. But what happens when a company becomes data-driven?

Well, first and foremost, they find ways to store all the data and make it accessible at all times.

This is when SQL comes in.

With SQL, you'll have a popular option due to its easy understandability and swiftness. The design of SQL is to mirror English in terms of written language and reading. As data is retrieved by way of SQL query, there will be no duplication. This is because data is accessed from its direct location thus allowing for a speedier process.

1.1 Historical Background and SQL Fundamentals

It wasn't until the 70s that saw the first introduction of SQL by Donald Chamberlin and Raymond Boyce. What they originally created was labeled as SEQUEL and mirrored a paper by Edgar Frank Todd that was published in early 1970. In Todd's paper, it was proposed that all of the database's data should be regarded as a relation. This was the theory used by Chamberlin and Boyce; thus, SQL was born. According to the book "Oracle Quick Guides," it states how SQL's original version was made to retrieve and manipulate stored data located in the original RDMI at IBM which was referred to as the "System R."

Then, as the years went by, SQL was eventually available to the public market. Shortly after this public release, the company known as Relational Software, better known as Oracle today, also offered a commercial version referred to as Oracle V2.

Ever since the ANSI and ISO decided to name SQL as the language standard for all communications of a database that are relational. Although there are many vendors who personalize the language to their own taste, their programs are still based on the approved SQL version adopted by ANSI.

SQL Fundamentals

SQL's proper pronunciation has always been disputable within the programming world. As far as the standard goes, the ANSI recognizes the SQL pronunciation as being "es queue el." Regardless, many programmers prefer to its pronunciation in the slang form of "sequel." However, you can call it by whatever feels good to you.

Although there are many varieties of SQL, the two most popular are used by the Oracle database and the Microsoft SQL Server. Microsoft SQL Server takes advantage of the Transact-SQL while Oracle utilizes its own PL/SQL. Even though these two variations are different, they are both used in conjunction with the SQL standard set by ANSI.

DDL and DML Sub-languages

There are two main sub-languages that SQL is divided into. The first is called DDL, and the other is known as DML. The other option, known as Data Definition Language or DDL, consists of a lot of commands that are best for database and database object creation and destruction. Once you've defined the structure of the database using DDL, then you can utilize the DML (Data Manipulation Language) for the modification, retrieval, and insertion of the data.

Commands of the Data Definition Language

This is the kind of language that can create and then destroy the database object as well as a database. The commands involved with a DDL are given the same treatment by database specialists as they set up or remove project database phases.

Below is a list of the commands:

1. Create

The "create" command is used to install a computer database management system (DMS) and manage other independent databases. For instance, if you want to maintain the contact information of customers for future reference or keep an employee database, then using the CREATE will make it happen.

2. Use

The "use" command enables you to choose which database to use as you utilize the DBMS.

Keep in mind the database you are currently working with so that the data will be manipulated properly by the SQL commands.

3. Alter

After using a database to make tables, it is possible that the definition will need to be changed. The "alter" command allows you to change anything in the table's structure without having to worry about recreating or deleting it.

4. Drop

The "drop" command permits you to "drop" or remove complete objects of the database from the DBMS. Caution should be exercised when using this command to avoid unintended and permanent removal of structures. If you plan to have single records dropped, then you can just "delete" them through the DML.

Data Manipulation Language Commands

We use the Data Manipulation Language (DML) for the retrieval, modification, and insertion of information found in a database. All users utilize the commands routinely during the database's operation.

1. **INSERT**

The SQL command "insert" is used when adding records to an existing table. For example, how HR would add employees that are new to their database system.

2. **SELECT**
3.
4. This one of the most used SQL command. The users of the database are allowed to obtain information that is specific from within a database that is operational.
5.
6. **UPDATE**

The "update," the command is used for modifying information contained in a table, both in individual and as bulk.

7. DELETE

With this command, you'll notice that its syntax is almost the same as other commands in the DML.

1.2 SQL Query Types

In the programming world, a question is formally referred to as a query. A query within a database can either be, action or select. With an action query, extra tasks are requested about information like deletion, refreshing, and addition, while a select query helps to recover information.

Queries are helpful devices when it comes to a database. A client uses them to obtain information, conduct different calculations and carry out a variety of database activities.

Luckily, Microsoft Access allows the implementation of several types of queries, where the main types involve the total, parameter, activity, and select queries. One can easily refer to them as another piece of the database – similar to a macro or table.

There are two simple ways of manufacturing a query in a database, that is:-

- Have the SQL queries scratch made manually or
- Use Microsoft Access's Query Wizard

Query Language

A query language is used in databases to create queries, and the standard that all others go by is the Microsoft Structured Query Language. Beneath this SQL umbrella, there are just a handful of language variations available, and these include NuoDB, Oracle SQL, and MySQL. Distinct databases also have question dialects such as XQuery, Data Mining Extensions, Neo4j's Cipher, and Cassandra Query Language (CQL) that are incorporated by the NoSQL databases and diagram databases.

Different agreements can also be obtained by the query. Basically, all queries that are used find information that is explicit by having explicit criteria separated. When this is done, the information can then be outlined or computed.

A variety of queries are also incorporated, including erase, refresh, to annex, influence table, crosstab, aggregates, and parameter. An example of this is when specific questions are run by a variety of parameter queries, then clients get prompted to add field values, and after that, it takes the incentive to help make criteria as a cluster query allows clients to summarize group data.

With a query database highlight, it also needs the ability to stockpile information. As a result, many query languages were also developed for different purposes and databases. However, the SQL remains to be the most understood and universal type. Honestly, many junior executives who deal with databases are surprised to hear that more than one query languages exist. The same way that children act surprised when they hear a foreign language for the first time. This bit of surprise for both scenarios may cause other languages to become comprehended.

When it comes to database basics, it is imperative to learn everything about SQL first, and you want to start with your "select" statement or "script" written first but minus a GUI (graphical user interface). With more and more relational databases utilizing a graphical user interface for the ease of managing a database, queries are now able to become a lot simpler to use with the tools, like the wizard known as drag-and-drop. Nevertheless, it is imperative to learn SQL due to the fact that the other tools will never have superior SQL power.

Select Query

This query type poses only an iota of difficulty when making an inquiry, consequently, making it the most commonly used in all databases of Microsoft Access. This utilization chooses the information that comes out of one of the table series that will then relay the required information.

Lastly, the client chooses the criteria to command the databases so that a determination can be found by the use of the criteria. After calling a select query, a table is created that allows you to change information to one record at a time.

Action Query

Once you call an activity question, results appear in the database based on what the query indicated. This allows several things to be incorporated including: creating new records, refreshing them, erasing lines, or creating a new table.

An action query is well-known throughout the information world due to its ability to change several records at once instead of just the normal one record, as we see in a "select query."

These are the four action query types available:

1. **Append Query** – this allows the addition of set consequences to an existing table.
2. **Update Query** – this allows for the refreshing of a table's field.
3. **Make Table Query** – this does exactly what its name suggests, a table is made based on a queries set consequences.
4. **Delete Query** – this will erase a hidden table's records from a query set result.

Parameter Query

When used in conjunction with Microsoft Access, a "parameter query" is able to use a variety of queries in order to achieve a desired outcome. Because of this, when a query like this is used, you are able to send parameters to the select or activity query. These can be a condition or esteem so that the query will know what needs to be completed explicitly.

With them being picked regardless of having an exchange box, the end-user will be able to enter any value in a parameter whenever they run a query. A parameter query is just a select query that has been altered.

Aggregate Query

An aggregate query is a unique type of query. It can make changes to other queries (like the parameter, activity, or choice) just like a parameter does it, but it's against a parameter passing to a different query and being aggregated with other fields chosen among other groups.

A summation is ultimately made within a table property that you choose. It can be turned into sums that are measurable, like a standard deviation or midpoints.

1.3 Database Advantages and Disadvantages

Advantages of a database include the following:

1. Redundancy in Data is controlled

In a normal data file system, the users maintain and handle their own group files.

This could cause the following problems:

- Data duplication in different file types

- Storage space is wasted due to duplicated stored data.

- The generation of errors caused by updating the exact data type of an unrelated file.

- Time gets wasted by re-entering data repeatedly.

- Needless use of computer resources

- Difficulty in combining information.

2. Inconsistency is eliminated

The information in an FPS ends up being duplicated all through the system. This leads to unnecessary repetition and data inconsistency. To overcome this, the duplicated data has to be removed from a multitude of files so inconsistency can be obliterated.

In order for this problem to be avoided, you will need a database that is centralized so that this information doesn't become conflicting.

As soon as the database has been centralized, any duplication will now be under control and free of any inconsistency.

3. Users receive better service

When using DBMS users expect better service delivery. However, in systems that are conventional information, availability is deficient and the retrieval of data extremely slow.

As soon as many of the conventional systems get integrated to create a database that is centralized, the information will be easily available, updated and shareable thanks to the DBMS commands.

When the data gets centralized inside a database, it also mean that a user will be able to receive information that is both combined and new that might otherwise have been inaccessible.

A DBMS can ease the interaction between programmers and users as compared to a system of file processing that a programmer might need in order to have new programs written for the demand to be met.

4. Improved system flexibility

Changes are sometimes needed for the stored data content in a system. This is easier through a centralized database instead of a conventional system.

Programs that run applications don't need changing or any alteration in the database data.

5. Improvement in integrity

With an organization's database data that is considered centralized with multiple users using it simultaneously, it's imperative to enforce integrity.

For a conventional system, because of the duplication of many files, changes or updates may inadvertently cause wrong data entry in a few of the files.

Whether or not the database is centralized, it could as well contain incorrect data. A few examples of this would be when a salary should have been entered as 1,000 but instead its 1,500 or when a student is shown as having borrowed materials from a library but is not even enrolled.

Both of these types of problems are avoidable if the procedures for validation are defined as soon as an operation for an update is made.

6. Standards are Enforceable

The standards can be easily enforced in a database system due to the entire database data being accessible via a DBMS that is centralized.

The standards here could also be relatable to the data format, data structure and data name.

Having data formats that are stored and standardized is often desirable in order for the migration of data in a system or interchange of data.

7. An Improvement in Security

In systems that are conventional, the developed applications are created in an impromptu way.

Frequently there are distinct organization systems that access various parts of data that are operational. In this type of environment, it can be a difficult task to enforce security.

When a database is set up, it is easier for security to be enforced because of centralized data.

It also allows for easier control of certain parts that are accessible in a database. Having various checks are then established for the different access types (delete, modify, retrieve) and database information.

8. Easy identification of organization requirement

Every organization is made up of departments or sections that may be competitors.

As soon as a centralized control setup is established for a database, it'll become mandatory for the organization's requirement to be identified as well as balancing any units of competition that arise.

This may negatively impact an organization if there is some conflict of interest.

9. Development of a model for data

The development of a model for data is probably the most significant advantage to have when a system database is getting set up in an organization. In systems that are conventional, it's highly probable that system files may get designed if certain demands are needed by an application.

Generally, the view is sometimes irrelevant. This is due to the fact that it won't be cost-effective for the organization's future.

10. Recovery and backup are provided

Databases that are centralized are able to provide backups and recoveries to help counter any problems that may occur due to any failures such as errors in the software, power failure, and disk crashes. When a recovery or backup is conducted, all of the current data becomes regenerated to a previous period that was unaffected by a failure.

Disadvantages of Database Systems

Database systems just like any other system out there they have their own shortcomings. Some of the major disadvantages include:

1. Complex Database

The database's system design is very complex, difficult to maneuver and time-consuming to get the job done.

2. Costs for software and hardware start-up are huge

There is a lot of investment necessary to have the proper software and hardware setup in order to maintain applications that are used.

3. All applications are susceptible to database damage

If a single database component becomes damaged or corrupted in any way, then all database applications become susceptible to damage as well. This is because all the applications rely on the database.

4. Costs for conversion are substantial

The costs for conversion can be pretty large if you want to move to database systems from a system that is file-based. This is due to the need for new techniques and unfamiliar tools.

5. Required training is necessary

All users and programmers must receive training. This includes the cost, time, and effort required to have all end-users fully trained and well prepared to use the database system.

Chapter 2:

Data Definition Language (DDL)

The main role of this type of language known as DDL, is to modify and create a structure related to objects in a database. These objects are made up of indexes, tables, schemes, and views.

A data definition language can also be referred to as a data description language in other circumstances, like how it can describe a table's records and fields within databases.

2.1 Data Definition Language for Table and Database Creation

A database's main components are tables. Tables allow the storage of information (that is related) to be retrieved whenever needed. Without tables, they would be no way to retrieve or store critical data within the database; thus, a database would not exist.

Tables can save personal details, such as: name, date of birth, address and job descriptions.

A table can relate to other tables, be used temporarily, or even be unrelated. Tables are also adjustable, and if the design is good, then it would be able to store concise and accurate information.

With SQL Server, there are three table types:

- Temporary tables – A hash-tag symbol describes them by including it at the beginning of the name. Other kinds that are temporary also have distinct scope levels.

- System tables– These are utilized internally by the server in order to have the objects of the database managed. They're identified by the characteristic **"sys"** name. So when you see "sysobjects" for example, this means that a database has an object list included in a table.

- User-defined tables – These are created by developers who intend to store information that is user-defined. They can be identified easily due to their user-defined status. Inside the Query Analyzer's Object Browser, they are listed separately and labeled "user" in the folder for main Tables.

But why exactly do we need tables? A table can be modeled on objects that exist in the real-world (bad guys, good guys, people, events or "activities").

If two tables are not related, it's hard to gain any beneficial data. It is equal to having a regular data file connected to a computer. However, when table relationships are defined, the stored data is informative and effective.

Relationships can be implemented among other tables by modeling their relationships through a scenario. For example, we can have a bad guy and a spy battle it out in order to prevent world dominance. Then, we will be able to model and implement the relationship inside the database to show the representation of what will happen.

A relationship can additionally help by enforcing the data's integrity. Following the relationship being defined by foreign and primary keys, we can define a table with a foreign key by having it only allowed having data rows if another table has its values.

Creating Databases by Using Data Definition Language (DDL)

With new Query Analyzer features, it is very easy to get a basic outline that will show objects of a database that are commonly needed. This can be accomplished with just a few clicks of the mouse and some programming know-how.

It's important to have a complete understanding of the "Create Database" statement, what to fill into the fields, and that way it's constructed equally as important as having the code entered.

In this section we will discuss the statement "Create Database" that SQL Server furnishes.

As mentioned before, the SQL is the basic language for all of the databases and it's used for data manipulation. It is made up of specific SQL pieces: DML and DDL.

The DML is utilized in the manipulation of database data. We know this because we are able to insert and delete new rows through DML. It's also easily seen due to an SQL statement beginning with Delete, Update, Insert, or Select.

The DDL is utilized for object creation in a database as well as defining the look of the data within a database. A DDL is also used for the creation of databases, views, and tables, as well deleting them. We can easily see the DDL due to its statement normally starting with the Drop, Alter, or Create.

With that in mind, you'll notice that a statement of Transact-SQL that got entered for database deletion is a nice mix of both DML and DDL.

This now lets us know what DML and DDL are made of. The statement Create Database can be difficult as it involves different variables that can be specified.

2.2 DDL Altering for Addition of Foreign Key

Foreign keys can be created in two different ways using a table with Oracle, that is: out-of-line and inline methods.

First of all, it is important to understand what a foreign key is.

When a constraint is put into tables, it is referred to as a foreign key. This enables you to make a specification concerning a table's column and points out a different table's primary key.

Data can be related by two other tables, this way data integrity is improved.

Below are the ways in which a foreign key can be created in an Oracle table.

Inline Constraint of Foreign Key

For foreign keys to be created with an inline constraint, you need to specify the keyword to create, the name of the table, and then have the brackets open. To make a column, you need to specify it as a foreign key and then insert References on its end.

You would then want to specify another table's name. This table will contain the necessary key that is considered the primary key that has to be linked over to the foreign key. For example, a departmental table that needs to create a table for the new employee including fields for department IDs, then a table labeled "other" would become the table for the department.

Note, you need to have the column name specified that will refer to the foreign key in the "other" table that is in the brackets. If the department and employee table is used, then the column would be named "department ID."

Lastly, you need to make sure that the table and columns are defined normally. The foreign key is going to be created as soon as the statement is run.

Out-of-line Constraint of Foreign Key

The second method of declaring the foreign key is with an out-of-line constraint.

Declaring the constraint this way is completed as soon as you declare the columns created.

The advantage of this method involves naming the foreign key, making it helpful to disable, enable, and alter later on. When using an inline method, you automatically generate a name through a database in Oracle.

To use the syntax of the foreign key's out-of-line method, you need to first have your columns and table name declared.

As soon as you declare the columns that are remaining in the bracket, then include a Constraint. Adding this will indicate the defining of a constraint

After this provide your constraint with a name. This name can be up-to 25 characters long.

If you want, you can go off the norm when naming your constraint.

Following the naming of the constraint, you can include Foreign Key for easy identification.

After that, leave the brackets open so that the table column name can be added to become the foreign key. When that is done, close the brackets.

Add References, and then the name of the other table that you need to refer to. This way, you create a table of employees and add Department IDs in order to identify a table in a department, then it would become the main department table.

Next, remove the brackets, add the column's name into the table (department table), then re-close the brackets.

Lastly, after the brackets are closed for the statement Create Table, add a semicolon. Now the statement's all set to be run. Your foreign key will have a name added as requested.

Now that you've learned how a foreign key is created and included in a table, all you have to do now is practice doing it.

2.3 DDL Foreign Key in Tables

This is a kind of key that will count as a constraint that can enforce the SQL's referential integrity of the server database. At least a few columns can be used for a link to be established between the two tables' data so that the data can be controlled as it gets stored inside a foreign key table.

Producing a constraint from a foreign key

In order for SQL constraints to be produced from a foreign key, the primary key will also have a column, which will be known as a constraint that is UNIQUE, and then we are able to find this in a table.

Here, we labeled the table "dept" as the parent table contains the Primary key that can get referenced as a "child" table so that it was put in with the foreign key.

Generate the foreign key without knowing about data that exists

Sometimes a referencing table could already exist including data that will violate the foreign key in SQL that you are planning to create.

If a constraint is created that has a check, it will create an error because of an already existing data that has violated the rule.

If creating a foreign key constraint is still on your mind, then you need to ignore the data that exists and have the rule validated by using "WITH NO CHECK." It will then be marked "not trusted" on the constraint

Having a foreign key created using the rules of UPDATE/DELETE

An SQL's foreign key can be created by having a "what" action specified in a reference table as update and delete occurs on a parent table's primary key. Here are a few examples.

- Action Not Needed – There will be no action needed if a delete or update fails in the column's primary key. If this occurs, then any change made goes back automatically.
- Set Default- This will set the value to the default on the column's foreign key as soon as there is a deleted or updated primary key value. If a defined default doesn't occur and the column becomes nullable, then you would set it to Null in the foreign key column. For the default constraint, it must be defined and nullable otherwise, an error happens, and the column for primary key gets restored a bit so that it is back in the state it was before.
- Setting Null – When you set null, you are setting the column for SQL's foreign key to the Null while the value for the primary key becomes a new value after being updated or deleted. If any of these kinds of null values are not supposed to be found in the column, then this specific column, the one for the delete/update of the primary key, will fail and give an error.

For a foreign key to be modified by the T-SQL, it's important that the foreign key constraint is dropped prior to creating any new changes.

For a foreign key to become disabled or enabled, you would use the following:

- A constraint for disabling – For the disabling to occur in the constraint of the SQL foreign key, a statement must be used to reflect that. You would then have the constraint and table's name replaced. Once the disabling of the foreign key is complete, the constraint will then be labeled as "not trusted."
- A constraint for enabling – In order to place the constraint back to its original place, you would need to alter the table and then check the constraint.

Having constraints enabled by checking data that exists.

In order to have a foreign key forced to check data that exists and have the constraint enabled, it is important to work with the statement for Alter Table along with the Constraint for Check and then Go.

2.4 DDL Unique Restraint in Tables

The "unique" constraint of the SQL server assures you of the uniqueness of data that is stored in one column or a column group. When working with a statement, it can easily have a table created that has unique data when compared to other parts of that specific table.

When working with the syntax that is following, you are going to define the constraint as "unique" inside a column constraint. The "unique" part of this is also going to be defined as a constraint in the table. For the syntax, you want to first create and label a table then insert an opening bracket then user ID Insert Primary Key Identity. Next, enter "Not Null" for first and last name. Enter an email as the unique and then close the brackets.

An index that is unique is going to be created in an automatic manner by the server because this is going to make sure that the enforcement is there for the stored data's uniqueness within the column that is part of a constraint that is already unique.
As a result, if an attempt is made to have a duplicate inserted into any row, it will be rejected by the SQL server and will give an error after rejecting it, saying there has been a violation of the constraint.

To have new rows inserted into a table, you need to enter "Insert Into" and then add your "values."
Although this statement has no problem working, this statement will fail because of having more than one email.

If your unique constraint doesn't have a separate name specified, the SQL server has no choice but to generate one automatically. For example, if we have a constraint name of Unique_person_example, although it won't be very legible.

To have a certain name assigned to the constraint, the constraint keyword needs to be used.

There are two benefits of having a name that is specific to a unique constraint:

- Its name can be referred to while the constraint is being modified

- Any error message can be easily classified

The Constraints that are Unique and Primary Key

You will find that the "unique constraint" that is there and its "primary key" are going to make sure that we see the uniqueness of the data, thus the unique constraint should be the ones used rather than the "primary key" if you are looking to have a single or multiple column's uniqueness enforced if they are not any column made up of the primary key,

This is not going to be the same as the constraints of PRIMARY KEY that we talked about earlier, but the constraints of UNIQUE will permit the value of NULL. In addition, these are going to be the constraints that will treat the value of NULL as a customary worth; in this way, it just permits one NULL for every section.

The accompanying statement embeds a line whose incentive the segment of the email that we are going to work with that is NULL:

INSERT INTO hr.persons(first_name, last_name)

VALUES ('John','Smith');

Presently, in the event that you attempt to embed one progressively NULL into the email segment, you will get a mistake:

INSERT INTO hr.persons(first_name, last_name)

VALUES ('Lily','Bush');

When we decide to go through and run all of this, the yield that we will be able to get out of it is going to be below:

1   Violation of UNIQUE KEY constraint 'UQ__persons__AB6E616417240E4E'. Can't embed copy key in object 'hr.persons.' The worth of the copy key here includes (<NULL>).

The point that we want to work with here is to characterize out the unique constraint so that we can then gather the segments up the way that we want. To do this, we want to be able to compose all of this as a table constraint that has the right section names, and that has commas in the right place for the whole process to work, like what we see in the following:

CREATE TABLE table_name (

key_column data_type PRIMARY KEY,

column1 data_type,

column2 data_type,

column3 data_type,

UNIQUE (column1,column2));

The model seen below is useful because it is responsible for making a constraint that is UNIQUE and it is made up of two segments that have to come in at once as well. This includes:

CREATE TABLE hr.person_skills (id INT IDENTITY PRIMARY KEY,person_id int, skill_id int, updated_at DATETIME, UNIQUE (person_id, skill_id)); This is a good part to work with because it will add in some of the constraints of UNIQUE to segments that already exist.

When it is time to take a new constraint that is UNIQUE and add it to the current segment, start gathering up the sections that are needed to the table you have. The SQL Server is initially going to take a look at the current information that is found in these segments to help in make sure that all of the qualities found are unique. In the event that SQL Server finds the copy esteems, at that point, it restores a mistake and doesn't take the time to add in this kind of constraint.

What we are going to see below is important because it is going to show us the structure of this kind of language, simply by adding in the constraint that we have been talking about to this table.

ALTER TABLE table_name

ADD CONSTRAINT constraint_name

UNIQUE(column1, column2,...);

To finish some of this up, we need to make the assumption that we are able to work with the table from HR below:

CREATE TABLE hr.persons (person_id INT IDENTITY PRIMARY KEY, first_name VARCHAR(255) NOT NULL, last_name VARCHAR(255) NOT NULL, email VARCHAR(255), telephone VARCHAR(20),);

The table that we have here will make sure that we are able to add in that constraint from before into the segment of the email.

ALTER TABLE hr. persons

ADD CONSTRAINT unique_email UNIQUE(email);

Along with this idea, the proclamation that shows up will make sure that we are able to add in this constraint not just to the emails that we are working with, but also to the telephone section if we would like.

ALTER TABLE hr.persons

ADD CONSTRAINT unique_phone UNIQUE(phone);

Delete UNIQUE constraints

There are a few things that we can do in order to make sure that we get the constraint of UNIQUE to work how we want. To do this, we need to utilize the articulation for ALTER TABLE DROP CONSTRAINT, just like we see below.

ALTER TABLE table_name

DROP CONSTRAINT constraint_name;

2.5 DDL Drop and Delete in Tables

There are going to be times when we want to work with the statement of DELETE. This is used in order to take away some of the lines that are on the table.

The structure for how this statement is going to look in SQL will include:

DELETE FROM table_name [WHERE condition];

table_name - the table name, which must be refreshed.

One thing to note here is that the statement of WHERE in this is going to delete in a discretionary direction, and make sure that it can distinguish the lines in the section that we want to delete.

In the event that you do end up excluding the WHERE condition, every one of the lines in this kind of table is deleted so it's important to be careful when going through and work with a DELETE question without adding in the provision for WHERE. A good example of how to work with this is below:

SQL DELETE Example

If we would like to go through and delete out the representative with ID of 100 out of our HR worker table, then we would need to go through and change up the code to look like the following (note that the WHERE statement is here as well).

DELETE FROM representative WHERE id = 100;

If we want to go through and delete out all of the columns that are in the table for our workers then we would need to change up the syntax that we are in to work with the following:

DELETE FROM representative;

SQL DROP Statement:

The next statement that needs emphasis is the one known as DROP. It is used to expel an article from the database. If you do this and drop one of your tables, this means that all the all the lines of the table were deleted so that the whole structure of the table would be expelled out of this database.

Keep in mind that when a table is fully dropped, it is gone permanently and the process is irreversible. If you want it back after this, you will need to redo it afresh.

When that table is dropped, all of the references that were put to the table will not be no longer be legitimate.

The syntax that we can work with to drop one of our tables in this language includes:

DROP TABLE table_name;

Below is an example to help you understand how to work with this statement.

If we want to drop the worker table, then we would need to go through and make a few changes like the following:

DROP TABLE worker;

You can utilize the $SYSTEM.SQL.DropTable() technique to delete a table in the current namespace. You indicate the SQL table name. In contrast to the DROP TABLE, this strategy can delete a table that was characterized without [DdlAllowed]. The subsequent contention determines whether the table information ought to likewise be deleted; as a matter of course, information isn't deleted.

DO $SYSTEM.SQL.DropTable("Sample.MyTable",1,.SQLCODE,. %msg)

In the event that SQLCODE '= 0 {WRITE "SQLCODE," blunder: ",%msg}

You can utilize the $SYSTEM.OBJ.Delete() strategy to delete at least one table in the current namespace. You should indicate the relentless class name that ventures the table (not the SQL table name). You can determine various class names utilizing trump cards. The subsequent contention indicates whether the table information ought to likewise be deleted; naturally, information isn't deleted.

Benefits
The DROP TABLE order is a favored activity. Before utilizing DROP TABLE. During this process, it is important for you to either work with the DROP_TABLE regulatory benefit, or you will need to work with the DELETE object benefit for

the table that is predetermined along the way. If you do not do this ahead of time, then you are going to end up with an error or another problem in your code. You can decide whether the present client has DELETE benefit by summoning the %CHECKPRIV order. You can decide whether a predetermined client has DELETE benefit by summoning the $SYSTEM.SQL.checkpoint() strategy. You can utilize the GRANT order to allot %DROP_TABLE benefits, on the off chance that you hold suitable giving benefits.

In inserted SQL, it is possible to work with the $SYSTEM.Security.Login() option so that you are able to sign in like one of the clients, and receive some of the many benefits in the process.:

DO $SYSTEM.Security.Login("_SYSTEM","SYS") &sql( )

Up until this point, you are probably going to have the %Service_Login: we are able to work with the benefit so that we can bring up our $SYSTEM.Security.Login strategy. To get ahold of some of the other crucial data, you should simply allude to %SYSTEM.Security in the InterSystems Class Reference.

DROP TABLE can't be utilized on a table made by characterizing a determined class, except if the table class definition incorporates [DdlAllowed].

8.3 Recovery Models

SQL Server recovery and backup activities happen inside the setting of the recuperation model of the database. Recuperation models are intended to control exchange log support. A recuperation model is a database property that controls how exchanges are logged, regardless of whether the exchange log requires (and permits) backing up, and what sorts of recovery activities are accessible. Three recuperation models exist: basic, full, and mass logged. Normally, a database utilizes the full recuperation model or basic recuperation model. A database can be changed to another recuperation model whenever the need arises.

8.4 Database Backup Methods

Three regular sorts of database reinforcements can be run on an ideal framework: ordinary (full), steady, and differential. Each type has points of interest and disservices, yet different database reinforcement approaches can be utilized together to structure a far-reaching server reinforcement and recuperation procedure. An altered reinforcement plan can limit personal time and amplify proficiency.

Before jumping into how every reinforcement functions and the upsides and downsides of each sort, it's essential to see how reinforcement programming tracks the different records that should be chronicled. At whatever point a document is made or refreshed, a file bit is connected to that record's filename. One can really see the file bit in that document's properties. The documented piece gets a checkmark whenever that record has been refreshed, and the reinforcement programming utilizes this checkbox to follow which documents on a framework are expected for filing.

Full or Ordinary Reinforcements

At the point when an ordinary or full reinforcement runs on a chose to drive, every one of the documents on that drive is supported up. This, obviously, incorporates framework documents, application records, client information — everything. Those records are then duplicated to the chose goal (reinforcement tapes, an auxiliary drive or the cloud), and all the file bits are then cleared.

Typical reinforcements are the quickest source to reestablish lost information since every one of the information on a drive is spared in one area. The drawback of ordinary reinforcements is that they set aside a long effort to run, and now and again, this is additional time than an organization can permit. Drives that hold a great deal of information may not be fit for a full reinforcement, regardless of whether they run medium-term. In these cases, steady and differential reinforcements can be added to the reinforcement timetable to spare time.

Steady Reinforcements

A typical method to manage the long-running occasions required for full reinforcements is to run them just on ends of the week. Numerous organizations, at that point, run gradual reinforcements during the time since they take far less time. A steady reinforcement will snatch just the documents that have been refreshed since the last ordinary reinforcement. When the gradual reinforcement has run, that record won't be shown up again except if it changes or during the following full reinforcement.

While steady database reinforcements do run quicker, the recuperation procedure is more convoluted. On the off chance that the ordinary reinforcement runs on Saturday and a record is, at that point, refreshed Monday morning, should something happen to that document on Tuesday, one would need to get to the Monday night reinforcement to reestablish it.

For one record, that is not very muddled. Be that as it may, should a whole drive be lost, one would need to reestablish the ordinary reinforcement in addition to every single other gradual reinforcement ran since the typical reinforcement.

Differential Reinforcements

An option in contrast to gradual database reinforcements that has a less confounded reestablish process is a differential reinforcement. Differential reinforcements and recuperation are like steady in that these reinforcements snatch just documents that have been refreshed since the last typical reinforcement. Be that as it may, differential reinforcements don't clear the chronicle bit. So a record that is refreshed after a typical reinforcement will be filed each time a differential reinforcement is run until the following ordinary reinforcement runs and clears the document bit.

Like our last model, if a typical reinforcement runs on Saturday night and a record gets changed on Monday, that document would then be supported up when the differential reinforcement runs Monday night. Since the file bit won't be cleared, even without any changes that record will keep on being replicated on the Tuesday night differential reinforcement and the Wednesday night differential reinforcement and each extra night until an ordinary reinforcement runs again catching all the drive's documents and resetting the file bit.

A reestablish of that record, if necessary, could be found in the earlier night's tape. In case of a total drive disappointment, one would need to reestablish the last ordinary reinforcement and just the most recent differential reinforcement. This is less tedious than a gradual reinforcement reestablish. Notwithstanding, every night that a differential reinforcement runs, the reinforcement documents get bigger, and the time it takes to run the reinforcement stretches.

Daily Reinforcements

There is a fourth, less regular type of reinforcement, known as daily. This is generally put something aside for strategic documents. In the event that documents that are refreshed always can't hold up an entire twenty-four hours for the daily backup to run and catch them, daily backups are the best decision. This sort of reinforcement utilizes the record's timestamp, not the file bit, to refresh the document once changes are made. This sort of database reinforcement runs during business hours, and having such a large number of these records can affect organized speeds.

8.5 Preparing to Restore the Database

While RMAN disentangles most databases, reestablishes and recuperates assignments, at present it's wise to arrange your database system dependent on which database records have been lost and your recuperation objective. This segment contains the accompanying points:

- Identifying the Database Records to Reestablish or Recuperate

- Determining the DBID of the Database

- Previewing Reinforcements Utilized in Reestablish Tasks

- Validating Reinforcements Before Reestablishing Them

- Restoring Chronicled Re-try Logs Required for Recuperation

- Distinguishing the Database Documents to Reestablish or Recuperate

The systems for figuring out which documents require to reestablish or recuperation rely on the sort of record that is lost.

Recognizing a Lost Control Record

It is typically clear when the control document of your database is lost. The database closes down quickly when any of the multiplexed control documents get distant. Likewise, the database reports a blunder on the off chance that you attempt to begin it without a legitimate control document at every area indicated in the CONTROL_FILES statement parameter.

Not all duplicates of your control record expect you to reestablish a control document from reinforcement. On the off chance that at any rate one control record stays flawless, then you can either duplicate an unblemished duplicate of the control document over the harmed or missing control record or update the introduction parameter record with the goal that it doesn't allude to the harmed or missing control record. After the CONTROL_FILES parameter references just present, unblemished duplicates, so of this specific document, it is possible to get the database to restart on its own.

On the off chance that you reestablish the control document from reinforcement, at that point, you should perform media recuperation of the entirety of the database, and then open it up when you already using the OPEN RESETLOGS choice, either way information records must be reestablished. This strategy is portrayed in "Performing Recuperation with a Reinforcement Control Record."

Distinguishing Data files Requiring Media Recuperation
When and how to recuperate relies upon the condition of the database and the area of its information records.
Recognizing Data files with RMAN
A simple strategy for figuring out which information documents are missing is to run an Approve DATABASE order, which endeavors to peruse every single indicated datum record. For instance, start the RMAN customer and run the accompanying directions to approve the database (test yield included).

8.6 Database Restore Types
You can reestablish up to the moment or reestablish to a past point in time in the accompanying circumstances:
- Restore to substitute way (area)

- Restore the Accessibility Gathering database

Reestablish up to the moment

In an authorized reestablish activity (choose by default), databases are recuperated up to the point of disappointment. This is cultivated by playing out the accompanying succession:

1. Backs up the last dynamic exchange log before reestablishing the database.

2. Restores the databases from the full database reinforcement that you select.

3. Applies all the exchange logs that were not dedicated to the databases (counting exchange logs from the reinforcements from the time the reinforcement was made up to the most current time).

Exchange logs are pushed forward and applied to any chosen databases.
An expert reestablish activity requires an adjacent arrangement of exchange logs.

Since the SnapCenter can't reestablish SQL Server database exchange logs from log-shipping reinforcement records (log-shipping allows you to send out your log reinforcements and exchange them, from one of your databases that are essential and found on one of your server occasions. This will get sent out to one or more of our auxiliary databases on one of the sever cases that are isolated or optional), you are not ready to play out an authorized reestablish activity from the exchange log reinforcements. Therefore, you should go through the SnapCenter to back your SQL Server database exchange log documents.

On the off chance that you don't have to hold regularly updated reestablish capacity for all reinforcements, you can arrange your framework's exchange log reinforcement maintenance through the reinforcement strategies.

Case of an authorized reestablish activity

Assuming that you run the SQL Server reinforcement consistently around early afternoon, and on Wednesday at 4:00 p.m., you have to reestablish from a reinforcement. For reasons unknown, the reinforcement from Wednesday early afternoon bombed check, so you choose to reestablish from the Tuesday early afternoon reinforcement. From that point onward, if the reinforcement is reestablished, all the exchange logs are pushed ahead and applied to the reestablished databases, beginning with those that were not dedicated when you made Tuesday's reinforcement and proceeding through the most recent exchange log composed on Wednesday at 4:00 p.m. (on the off chance that the exchange logs were upheld).

Reestablish to a past point in time

In a point-in-time reestablish activity, databases are reestablished distinctly to a particular time from an earlier time. A point-in-time reestablish activity happens in the accompanying reestablish circumstances:

- The database is reestablished to a given time in an upheld up exchange log.
- The database is reestablished, and just a subset of upheld up exchange logs are applied to it.

8.7 Detaching and Attaching Database

The information and exchange log documents of a database can be separated and afterward reattached to the equivalent or another case of SQL Server. Separating and appending a database is valuable in the event that you need to change the database to an alternate occasion of SQL Server on a similar PC or to move the database.

Separating a database expels it from the case of SQL Server however leaves the database flawless inside its information documents and exchange log records. These records would then be utilized to connect the database to any case of SQL Server, including the server from which the database was disconnected.

You can't disconnect a database if any of the following is valid:

- The database is imitated and distributed. In case it's repeated, the database must be unpublished.

Before confining it, you should cripple distributing by running sp_replicationdboption.

- A database preview exists on the database.
- Before disengaging the database, you should drop the entirety of its depictions.
- The database is being reflected in a database reflecting session.
- The database can only be confined if the session is ended. Failure to do that then the database is suspect. A speculate database can't be separated; before confining it, you should place it into crisis mode. The database is a framework database.

Backup and Restore and Detach

Detaching a read-just database loses data about the differential bases of differential backups.

Reacting to Detach Error
Errors delivered while detaching a database can keep the database from shutting neatly and the exchange log from being remade. In the event that you get a blunder message, play out the accompanying remedial activities:

1. Reattach all records related to the database, not simply the essential document.
2. Resolve the issue that caused the blunder message.

3. Detach the database once more.

Joining a Database

You can join a replicated or detached SQL Server database. At the point when you connect a SQL Server 2005 (9.x) database that contains full-content list records onto a SQL server case, the inventory documents are joined from their past area alongside the other database documents, equivalent to in SQL Server 2005 (9.x). For more data, see *Redesign Full-Content Inquiry.*

Whenever you append a database, all information records (MDF and NDF documents) must be accessible. In the event that any information document has an alternate way from when the database was first made or last appended, you should indicate the present format of the record.

In the event that a scrambled database is first connected to an example of SQL Server, the database proprietor must open the ace key of the database by executing the accompanying articulation: OPEN Ace KEY Decoding BY Secret key = 'secret word.' We prescribe that you allow programmed decoding of the ace key by executing the accompanying proclamation: Adjust Ace KEY Include ENCRYPTION BY Administration Ace KEY. For more data, see Make Ace KEY (Execute SQL) and Change Ace KEY (Execute SQL).

The necessity for joining log records depends somewhat on whether the database is perused compose or read-just, as explained below:

- For a read-compose database, you can, for the most part, append a log record in another area. Be that as it may, now and again, reattaching a database requires its current log documents. Consequently, it is critical to consistently keep all the detached log records until the database has been effectively appended without them.
- In the event that a read-compose database has a solitary log document and you don't indicate another area for the log record, the connect activity searches in the old area for the document. In the event that it is discovered, the old log document is utilized, paying little heed to whether the database was closed down neatly. However, if the old log document isn't found and if the database was closed down neatly and has no dynamic log chain, the join activity endeavors to fabricate another log record for the database.
- If the essential information record being joined is just perused, the Database Motor expects that the database is perused as it were. For a read-just database, the log document or records must be accessible at the area determined in the essential document of the database. Another log record

can't be manufactured on the grounds that SQL Server can't refresh the log area put away in the essential document.

Changes in Metadata when Attaching Databases

When a read-just database is detached and afterward reattached, the backup data about the present differential base is lost. The differential base is the latest full backup of the considerable number of information in the database or in a subset of the records or file groups of the database. Without the base-backup data, the ace database gets unsynchronized with the read-just database, so differential backups taken from that point may give surprising outcomes. Consequently, in the event that you are utilizing differential backups with a read-just database, you ought to build up another differential base by taking a full backup after you reattach the database.

On append, database startup happens. Appending a database places it in a similar state that it was in when it was detached or duplicated. Regardless, connect and-detach activities both impair cross-database proprietorship anchoring for the database.

Backup and Restore and Join

Like any database that is completely or somewhat disconnected, a database with reestablishing records can't be connected. On the off chance that you stop the restore arrangement, you can append the database. At that point, you can restart the restore grouping.

Joining a Database to Another Server Occurrence
When you join a database onto another server occurrence, to give a predictable encounter to clients and applications, you may need to re-make a few or the entirety of the metadata for the database, for example, logins and occupations, on the other server case.

Existing Object Privileges

Note that, erasing one of our tables isn't going to go through and delete the article benefits for that table at the same time. For example, the benefit that is given over to a client in order to delete or update that table will remain the same. This is going to provide us with one out of two options that include:

1. If we delete the table and then we make a table that comes in with a similar name, the clients and the jobs that are placed on this are going to have some of the same benefits to the new table compared to what was present in the old table.
2. Once you delete one of the tables, it is going to be kind of silly to expect to repudiate the benefits of the object for this table.

This means that, before working with the REVOKE, always order to take the objects from one table and then save them before you decide to erase that table.

Table Containing Data

As a matter of fact, DROP TABLE deletes the table definition and will help us to delete the information of the table. If you work with the DROP TABLE command and it works with some information that is not set up to be deleted, such as our referential constraint, then any of the information that you erased before is going to be erased in this as well.

In order to set up the default framework, make sure that it is set up to work with the information to delete the table. Assume that the wide default is part of the framework and that it is set to not delete the information in the table, we can delete out the information for all of the tables by determining the DROP TABLE using that command. As shown below:

- The $SYSTEM.SQL.SetDDLDropTabDelData() strategy call. If you would like to go through and decide what the present settings should be, we will call up $SYSTEM.SQL.CurrentSettings(), which is really useful because it will show us that the DROP TABLE command is able to delete the information setting.

- The default is "Yes" (1). This is usually the method that is recommended to go with because the other option is "No" (0) in the event that you need work with the command of DROP TABLE so that you don't end up getting rid of all the information of the table when the definition of the table is gone.

- You can utilize the TRUNCATE TABLE direction to delete the table's information without erasing the table definition.

Lock Applied

The DROP TABLE statement is going to be a good one to work with because it helps to secure a lock on your table. This is going a great way to keep the procedures you have in the table from making any changes to the definition of the table information if you are working with a table cancellation as well. This table-level lock is adequate for erasing both the table definition and the table information; DROP TABLE doesn't procure a lock on each line of the table information. This is a good lock to work with because it will be discharged in an automatic manner near the end of the DROP TABLE activity.

Remote Key Constraints

The next thing that we need to look at is the Remote Key Constraints. We are not able to drop one of our tables if there are any constraints that are characterized on one of the other tables that reference back to the table that you hope to drop in the process. This means that we need to go through and remove the references before we try to do this at all.

Related Queries

Dropping a table consequently cleanses any related reserved inquiries and cleanses question data as put away in %SYS.PTools.SQLQuery. Dropping a table naturally cleanses any SQL runtime measurements (SQL Stats) data for any related inquiry.

Nonexistent Table

To decide whether a predetermined table exists in the current namespace, utilize the $SYSTEM.SQL.TableExists() strategy.

In the event that you attempt make changes to a table that is not there or that you have not been able to create yet, DROP TABLE issues an SQLCODE – 30 mistakes, of course. Either way, this mistake revealing conduct is there when we work by setting the arrangement of the framework is shown below:

- The $SYSTEM.SQL.SetDDLNo30() strategy call. To decide the present setting, call $SYSTEM.SQL.CurrentSettings(), which shows a Suppress SQLCODE=-30 Errors: setting.

- The next thing that we need to do is get to our management portal. From there, select [Home] > [Configuration] > [General SQL Settings]. This is going to allow us to view the setting that we are on right now for our DDL DROP on one of the views or tables that are non-existent.

The default that we are able to see with this one is "No" (0). This is the prescribed setting for this alternative. Of course, we can also work with "Yes" (1) on the off chance that you need a command of DROP TABLE for one of the tables that is nonexistent to play out and will not receive any kind of error message.

4.6   DDL to Create Views

To make another view show up in the server that you are creating, you just need to work with the statement CREATE VIEW as demonstrated as follows:

CREATE VIEW [OR ALTER] schema_name.view_name
[(column_list)]
AS
select_statement;

Looking at the command structure above, we will notice that:

- First, to determine the name that we want to this view. This is going to simply show off the name of our schema and our composition where we are placing our view.

- The second thing that we will work on is using the statement of SELECT that will help us to characterize our view, but we are going to work with the catchphrase AS. The SELECT statement can sometimes allude to one or more table.

- In the event that you are not going to indicate the sections that you would like to see with the view you are on, then this server is going to utilize the

> list segment that it was able to bring up when working with the statement SELECT.
> - If you do end up in a situation where you need to reclassify the view, or you would like to expel or add a few more parts to it, you can work with the statement OR ALTER after you are done working with CREATE VIEW.

SQL Server CREATE VIEW models

The next thing that we need to work with is the CREATE VIEW models that are available. With this one, we are going to work with items from our tables and the order_items. Making a straightforward view model is going to help us to get things done.

The statement that we are going to work with below will help us to take a look at the daily sales that a company has, and it will be based on the requests, the items, and the order_items tables that available.

Once we are able to work with the table for daily sales and that is all set up in the proper manner, we can make an inquiry against some of the basic tables, to make this happen we'll only work with the SELECT statement. The syntax seen when working with this kind of code is shown below:

```
SELECT
*
FROM

sales.daily_sales
```

Request BY

y, m, d, product_name;

Rethinking the view model
We can take this a bit further and add in the names of our clients to the desired part of the table. To do this, we can work with the command CREATE or the OR ALTER option. A good example of the code that we are using to make this one work includes:

```
CREATE OR ALTER sales.daily_sales (
year, month, day,
customer_name,
product_id, product_name deals )
AS
SELECT
year(order_date),
month(order_date),
day(order_date),
concat(
first_name,
' ',
last_name
),
p.product_id,
product_name,
amount * i.list_price
FROM
sales.orders AS o
Internal JOIN
```

```
sales.order_items AS I
ON o.order_id = i.order_id
Internal JOIN
production.products AS p

ON p.product_id = i.product_id

Internal JOIN sales.customers AS c

ON c.customer_id = o.customer_id;
```

Chapter 3:

Ensuring the Integrity of Data

The term information honesty alludes to the precision and consistency of information.

While making databases, consideration should be given to information uprightness and how to look after it. A decent database will authorize information trustworthiness at whatever point conceivable.

For instance, a client could coincidentally attempt to enter a telephone number into a date field. In the event that the framework authorizes information honesty, it will keep the client from committing these errors.

Keeping up information respectability implies ensuring the information stays flawless and unaltered all through its whole life cycle. This incorporates the catch of the information, stockpiling, refreshes, moves, reinforcements, and so on. Each time information is prepared, there's a hazard that it could get debased (regardless of whether inadvertently or malevolently).

Dangers to Data Integrity

Information honesty is in danger when:

- A client attempts to enter a date outside a satisfactory range.

- A client attempts to enter a telephone number in an inappropriate format.

- A bug in an application tries to delete an inappropriate record.

- While moving information between two databases, the designer coincidentally attempts to embed the information into an inappropriate table.

- While moving information between two databases, the system went down.

- A client attempts to delete a record in a table, yet another table is referencing that record as a component of a relationship.

- A client attempts to refresh an essential key worth when there's a remote key in a related table indicating that worth.

-
- A designer overlooks that he's on a generation framework and starts entering test information legitimately into the database.

- A programmer figures out how to take all client passwords from the database.

- A programmer hacks into the system and drops the database (for example, deletes it and every one of its information).

- Fire moves through the structure, reducing the database PC to ashes.

- When the normal reinforcements of the database have been coming up short for as far back as two months.

The list of instances where information trustworthiness is in danger goes on.

A considerable lot of these dangers can be addressed from inside the database itself (using information types and constraints against every segment, for instance, encryption, and so on), while others can be addressed through different highlights of the DBMS, (for example, customary reinforcements – and testing that the reinforcements do really reestablish the database true to form).

A portion of these require other (non-database related) elements to be available, for example, an offsite reinforcement area, an appropriately working IT arrange, legitimate preparing, security strategies, and so on.

4 Types of Data Integrity

In the database world, information trustworthiness is regularly put into the accompanying sorts:

- Entity trustworthiness

- Referential trustworthiness

- Domain trustworthiness

- User-characterized trustworthiness

Substance Integrity

Substance honesty characterizes each line to be unique inside its table. No two columns can be the equivalent.

To accomplish this, an essential key can be characterized. The essential key field contains a unique identifier – no two columns can contain a similar unique identifier.

Referential Integrity

Referential integrity is concerned about connections.
When at least two tables have a relationship, we need to
guarantee that the remote key worth matches the
essential key an incentive consistently. We would rather
not have a case where a remote key worth has no
coordinating essential key to an incentive in the essential
table. This would bring about a stranded record.

Hence referential honesty will keep clients from:

- Adding records to a related table if there is no
  related record in the essential table.

- Changing values in an essential table that outcome
  in stranded records in a related table.

- Deleting records from an essential table if there are
  coordinating related records.

Domain Integrity

Domain integrity concerns the legitimacy of sections for a given segment. Choosing the suitable information type for a segment is the initial phase in keeping up domain integrity. Different advances could incorporate, setting up fitting constraints and rules to characterize the information position and additionally limiting the scope of potential qualities.

User-Defined Integrity
User-defined integrity enables the user to apply business decides to the database that isn't secured by any of the other three information integrity types.

3.1 The Basics of Integrity Constraints

Next we will look at the Integrity constraints. These are used when applying some of the business rules on all of the tables for a database. They are accessible with the help of the Foreign key, and there are a few ways that we are able to define these, including:

1. The first option will be determining the constraints with the help of the definition of the section. This is often known as the level definition.
2. We can also define the constraints after each of the segments has gone through the right definition. This will be the definition that is table level.
3.

Next, let's look at what is a SQL Primary key. This is a special kind of constraint that helps to characterize a section or even a blend of some of the segments we have that will be able to uniquely recognize each line in the table. This will help in ensuring that the constraints are done the desired way. For example:

- column_name1, column_name2 w.

Will be the names that will be used to work on the primary key constraint or the essential key.

- The linguistic structure inside the section, for example [CONSTRAINT constraint_name], is discretionary.

In order to ensure that we are able to create a table for work that uses the constraint of the primary key, the question would need to resemble this as well. Let's work on an example

This is going to be a constraint that we are able to work with to help distinguish any of the segments that reference back to the specific PRIMARY KEY that is found in one of our other tables. In fact, it is going to help us set up the connection that we need between two segments that fall between similar tables as well.

In order to define one of our sections as this foreign key, we need to make sure that we first define it as it is the Primary Key to our table that we are alluding back to. This will allow us to find a minimum of one segment that we can define as the Foreign key. The syntax that we are working with here will include:

The language structure to characterize one of our Foreign key when we get to the section level is:

[CONSTRAINT   constraint_name]   REFERENCES Referenced_Table_name(column_name)

Language structure to characterize a Foreign key at table level:

[CONSTRAINT   constraint_name]   FOREIGN KEY(column_name)   REFERENCES referenced_table_name(column_name);

For Example:

1) Let's utilize the "item" table and "order_items."

Foreign Key at section level:

Make TABLE item

(product_id number(5) CONSTRAINT pd_id_pk PRIMARY KEY,

product_name char(20),
supplier_name char(20),

unit_price number(10)

);

Make TABLE order_items

(order_id number(5) CONSTRAINT od_id_pk PRIMARY KEY,

product_id number(5) CONSTRAINT
    pd_id_fkREFERENCES,
product(product_id), product_name char(20),
supplier_name char(20), unit_price number(10));

Foreign Key at table level:

Make TABLE order_items (order_id number(5) ,
product_id number(5), product_name char(20),
supplier_name char(20), unit_price number(10)

CONSTRAINT od_id_pk PRIMARY
KEY(order_id),CONSTRAINT pd_id_fk FOREIGN
KEY(product_id) REFERENCES product(product_id));

2) If the representative table has a 'mgr_id' i.e, supervisor id as a foreign key which references essential key 'id' inside a similar table, the question would resemble,

Make TABLE representative (id number(5) PRIMARY KEY, name char(20), dept char(10), age number(2), mgr_id number(5) REFERENCES employee(id), compensation number(10), area char(10));

3) SQL Not Null Constraint:

This constraint guarantees all lines in the table contain a positive incentive for the section, which is indicated as not invalid. Which implies an invalid worth isn't permitted.

Linguistic structure to characterize a Not Null constraint:

[CONSTRAINT constraint name] NOT NULL

For Example: To make a work table with Null worth, the inquiry would resemble

Make TABLE worker

(id number(5),

name char(20) CONSTRAINT nm_nn NOT NULL, dept char(10),

age number(2),

pay number(10),

area char(10)

);

4) SQL Unique Key:

This constraint guarantees that a section or a gathering of segments in each line has an unmistakable worth. A column(s) can have an invalid worth, yet the qualities can't be copied.

Sentence structure to characterize a Unique key at section level:

[CONSTRAINT constraint_name] UNIQUE

Sentence structure to characterize a Unique key at table level:

[CONSTRAINT constraint_name] UNIQUE(column_name)

For Example: To make a work table with Unique key, the inquiry would resemble,

Unique Key at section level:

Make TABLE worker

(id number(5) PRIMARY KEY,

```
name char(20),

dept char(10),

age number(2),

pay number(10),

area char(10) UNIQUE

);
```

or on the other hand

```
Make TABLE worker

( id number(5) PRIMARY KEY,

name char(20),

dept char(10),

age number(2),

pay number(10),

area char(10) CONSTRAINT loc_un UNIQUE

);
```

Unique Key at table level:

Make TABLE worker

(id number(5) PRIMARY KEY,

name char(20),

dept char(10),

age number(2),

pay number(10),

area char(10),

CONSTRAINT loc_un UNIQUE(location)

);

5) SQL Check Constraint:

This constraint characterizes a business rule on a section. Every one of the lines must fulfill this standard. The constraint can be applied for a solitary section or a gathering of segments.

Linguistic structure to characterize a Check constraint:

[CONSTRAINT constraint_name] CHECK (condition)

For Example: In the worker table to choose the sexual orientation of an individual, the inquiry would resemble

Check Constraint at section level:

Make TABLE worker

(id number(5) PRIMARY KEY,

name char(20),

dept char(10),

age number(2),

sexual orientation char(1) CHECK (sex in ('M','F')),

pay number(10),

area char(10)

);

Check Constraint at table level:

Make TABLE worker

(id number(5) PRIMARY KEY,

name char(20),

dept char(10),

age number(2),

sexual orientation char(1),

pay number(10),

area char(10),

CONSTRAINT gender_ck CHECK (sexual orientation in ('M','F'))

);

3.2 Check Constraint

In this segment, we will disclose how to utilize the check constraints in SQL Server (Transact-SQL) with linguistic structure and models.

What makes up an SQL Server check constraint?

A check constraint in SQL Server (Transact-SQL) enables you to indicate a condition on each line in a table.

Note

- A check constraint can NOT be defined on a SQL View.

- The check constraint defined on a table must allude to just sections in that table. It cannot allude to segments in different tables.

- A check constraint can exclude a Subquery.

- A check constraint can be defined in either a CREATE TABLE statement or an ALTER TABLE statement.

*Utilizing a **CREATE TABLE** statement*

The language structure for making a check constraint utilizing a CREATE TABLE statement in SQL Server (Transact-SQL) is:

Make TABLE table_name

(

column1 datatype [NULL | NOT NULL],

column2 datatype [NULL | NOT NULL], ...

CONSTRAINT constraint_name

CHECK [NOT FOR REPLICATION] (column_name condition)

);

table_name

The name of the table that you wish to make with a check constraint.

constraint_name

The name to allocate to the check constraint.

column_name

The segment in the table that the check constraint applies to.

Condition

The condition that must be met for the check constraint to succeed.

Model

Let's have a look at how to utilize the CREATE TABLE statement in SQL Server to make a check constraint.

For example:

Make TABLE representatives

(employee_id INT NOT NULL,

last_name VARCHAR(50) NOT NULL,

first_name VARCHAR(50),

compensation MONEY,

CONSTRAINT check_employee_id

CHECK (employee_id BETWEEN 1 and 10000)

```
);
```

In this first model, we've made a check constraint on the representative's table called check_employee_id. This constraint guarantees that the employee_id field contains values somewhere in the range of 1 and 10000.

We should investigate another model..

Make TABLE representatives

(employee_id INT NOT NULL,

last_name VARCHAR(50) NOT NULL,

first_name VARCHAR(50),

compensation MONEY,

CONSTRAINT check_salary

CHECK (compensation > 0)

);

In this subsequent model, we've made a check constraint on the representative's table called check_salary. This constraint guarantees that the pay esteem is more prominent than 0.

Utilizing an ALTER TABLE statement

The language structure for making a check constraint in an ALTER TABLE statement in SQL Server (Transact-SQL) is:

ALTER TABLE table_name

ADD CONSTRAINT constraint_name

CHECK (column_name condition);

table_name

The name of the table that you wish to change by adding a check constraint.

constraint_name

The name to allocate to the check constraint.

column_name

The segment in the table that the check constraint applies to.

Condition

The condition that must be met for the check constraint to succeed.

Model

Let's have a glance at how to utilize the ALTER TABLE statement to make a check constraint in SQL Server.

For instance:

ALTER TABLE workers

ADD CONSTRAINT check_last_name

CHECK (last_name IN ('Smith', 'Anderson', 'Jones'));

In this model, we've made a check constraint on the current worker's table called check_last_name. It guarantees that the last_name field just contains the accompanying qualities: Smith, Anderson, or Jones.

Drop a Check Constraint

The sentence structure for dropping a check constraint in SQL Server (Transact-SQL) is:

ALTER TABLE table_name

DROP CONSTRAINT constraint_name;

table_name

The name of the table that you wish to drop the check constraint.

constraint_name

The name of the check constraint to expel.

Model

Let's have a look at how to drop a check constraint in SQL Server.

For instance:

ALTER TABLE representatives

DROP CONSTRAINT check_last_name;

In this SQL Server model, we are dropping a check constraint on the representative's table called check_last_name.

Empower a Check Constraint

The language structure for empowering a check constraint in SQL Server (Transact-SQL) is:

ALTER TABLE table_name

WITH CHECK CONSTRAINT constraint_name;

table_name

The name of the table that you wish to empower the check constraint.

constraint_name

The name of the check constraint to empower.
Model

Let's have a look at how to empower a check constraint in SQL Server.

For instance:

ALTER TABLE representatives

WITH CHECK CONSTRAINT check_salary;

In this model, we are empowering a check constraint on the representative's table called check_salary.

Handicap a Check Constraint

The linguistic structure for crippling a check constraint in SQL Server (Transact-SQL) is:

ALTER TABLE table_name

NO CHECK CONSTRAINT constraint_name;

table_name

The name of the table that you wish to handicap the check constraint.

constraint_name

The name of the check constraint to handicap.
Model

Let's take a look at how to cripple a check constraint in SQL Server.

For instance:

ALTER TABLE workers

NO CHECK CONSTRAINT check_salary;

In this SQL Server model, we are impairing a check constraint on the representative's table called check_salary.

3.3 Unique Constraint

This section talks about how to make, add, and drop unique constraints in SQL Server with linguistic structure and models.

What is a unique constraint in SQL Server?

A unique constraint is a solitary field or mix of fields that uniquely characterizes a record. A portion of the fields can contain invalid qualities as long as the blend of qualities is unique.

What is the contrast between a unique constraint and an essential key?

Essential Key Unique Constraint

None of the fields that are a piece of the essential key can contain an invalid value.

Some of the fields that are a part of the unique constraint can contain invalid qualities as long as the mix of qualities is unique.

Make unique Contraint - Using a CREATE TABLE statement

The sentence structure for making a unique constraint utilizing a CREATE TABLE statement in SQL Server is:

Make TABLE table_name

(

column1 datatype [NULL | NOT NULL],

column2 datatype [NULL | NOT NULL], ...

CONSTRAINT constraint_name UNIQUE (uc_col1, uc_col2, ... uc_col_n)

);

table_name

The name of the table that you wish to make.

column1, column2

The sections that you wish to make in the table.

constraint_name

The name of the unique constraint.

uc_col1, uc_col2, ... uc_col_n

The segments that make up the unique constraint.

Model

Let's take a glance at how to make a unique constraint in SQL Server utilizing the CREATE TABLE statement.

Make TABLE representatives

(employee_id INT PRIMARY KEY,

employee_number INT NOT NULL, last_name VARCHAR(50) NOT NULL, first_name VARCHAR(50), compensation MONEY, CONSTRAINT employees_unique UNIQUE (employee_number));

In this model, we've made a unique constraint on the representative's table called employees_unique. It comprises of just one field which is the employee_number.

We could also make a unique constraint with more than one field as in the model beneath:

Make TABLE workers

(employee_id INT PRIMARY KEY,

employee_number INT NOT NULL,

last_name VARCHAR(50) NOT NULL,

first_name VARCHAR(50),

pay MONEY,

CONSTRAINT employees_unique UNIQUE (last_name, first_name)

);

Make unique constraint - Using an ALTER TABLE statement

The linguistic structure for making a unique constraint utilizing an ALTER TABLE statement in SQL Server is:

ALTER TABLE table_name

ADD CONSTRAINT constraint_name UNIQUE (column1, column2, ... column_n);

table_name

The name of the table to alter. This is the table that you wish to add a unique constraint to.

constraint_name

The name of the unique constraint.

column1, column2, ... column_n

The sections that make up the unique constraint.

Model

Let's have a look at how to add a unique constraint to a current table in SQL Server utilizing the ALTER TABLE statement.

ALTER TABLE representatives

ADD CONSTRAINT employees_unique UNIQUE (employee_number);

In this model, we've made a unique constraint on the current representative's table called employees_unique. It comprises of the field called employee_number.

We could likewise make a unique constraint with more than one field as in the model beneath:

ALTER TABLE representatives

ADD CONSTRAINT employee_name_unique UNIQUE (last_name, first_name);

Drop Unique Constraint

The sentence structure for dropping a unique constraint in SQL Server is:

ALTER TABLE table_name

DROP CONSTRAINT constraint_name;

table_name

The name of the table to change. This is the table whose unique constraint you wish to evacuate.
constraint_name

The name of the unique constraint to evacuating.

Model

Let's look at how to expel a unique constraint from a table in SQL Server.
ALTER TABLE workers

DROP CONSTRAINT employees_unique;

In this model, we're dropping a unique constraint on the worker's table called employees_unique.

3.4 Not Null Constraint

The NOT NULL constraint avoids embeddings NULL qualities into a segment. In the database world, NULL methods obscure or missing data.

When a NOT NULL constraint is applied to a segment, while attempting to embed a NULL incentive into or update NULL incentive from the section, the database motor will dismiss the change and issue a mistake.

You can make a NOT NULL constraint in making or altering the table.

Making SQL NOT NULL constraints

The most well-known approach to make a NOT NULL constraint is through the segment's meaning of the CREATE TABLE statement. For instance, the accompanying statement makes another table named creators:

CREATE TABLE creators(

author_id INT(11) NOT NULL AUTO_INCREMENT PRIMARY KEY,

author_name VARCHAR(40) NOT NULL,

bio VARCHAR(400) NULL

)

We've applied the NOT NULL constraints to the author_id and author_name sections.

In the event that you need to add a NOT NULL constraint to a section of a current table, you need to utilize the ALTER TABLE statement as pursues:

ALTER table

ALTER COLUMN section NOT NULL;

For instance, we can add a NOT NULL constraint to the bio section in Microsoft SQL Server:

ALTER TABLE creators

ALTER COLUMN BIO VARCHAR(400) NOT NULL;

In MySQL:

ALTER TABLE creators

Alter BIO VARCHAR(400) NOT NULL;

In Oracle:

ALTER TABLE creators MODIFY bio NOT NULL

Expelling SQL NOT NULL constraint

To expel a current NOT NULL constraint, you utilize the ALTER TABLE statement. For instance, to expel the NOT NULL constraint on the bio segment, you utilize the accompanying statement:

In SQL Server:

ALTER TABLE creators

ALTER COLUMN bio varchar(400) NULL

In MySQL:

ALTER TABLE creators

Change BIO VARCHAR(400) NULL;

In Oracle:

ALTER TABLE creators

Change (bio NULL)

In this instructional exercise, we have covered the best way to apply SQL NOT NULL constraint to anticipate adding NULL qualities to segments of a table.

3.5 Foreign Key Constraint

A foreign key is a segment (or mix of sections) in a table whose qualities must match estimations of a segment in some other table. The motivation behind foreign keys is to authorize referential integrity, which basically says that in the event that section esteem A alludes to segment esteem B, at that point, segment esteem B must exist.

For instance, given a request table and a client's table, in the event that you make a segment order .customer_id that references the customers.id essential key:

- Each esteem embedded or refreshed in orders.customer_id should precisely coordinate an incentive in customers.id, or be NULL.

- Values in customers.id that is referenced by orders.customer_id can't be deleted or refreshed, except if you have falling activities. Be that as it may, estimations of customers.id that are absent in orders.customer_id can be deleted or refreshed.

Rules for making foreign keys

Foreign Key Columns

- Foreign key sections must utilize their referenced segment's sort.

- Each section can't have a place with more than 1 Foreign Key constraint.

- It cannot be a registered segment.

- Foreign key sections must be ordered. This is required on the grounds that updates and deletes on the referenced table should look at the referencing table for any coordinating records to guarantee those activities would not disregard existing references. By and by, such lists are likely likewise required by applications utilizing these tables, since discovering all records which have a place with some substance, for instance, all requests for a given client, are exceptionally normal.

NOTE: To meet this necessity while making another table, there are a couple of alternatives:

➤ New in v19.1: A record on the referencing sections is consequently made for you when you add a foreign key constraint to a vacant table if a suitable list doesn't exist. For a model, see Add the foreign key constraint with CASCADE.

➤ Create files unequivocally utilizing the INDEX condition of CREATE TABLE.

➤ Rely on some of the files that will rely on the constraints of UNIQUE or PRIMARY KEY.

➤ Have Cockroach DB consequently make a file of the foreign key that you would like to work with. However, it is important to remember on the off chance that you later expel the Foreign Key constraint; this consequently made file isn't evacuated.

➤ This allows us to work with the sections of our foreign keys as a kind of prefix of a record's segments likewise fulfills the necessity for a file. For instance, in the event that you make some of the segments of your foreign key, which would be A and B, and then we would have a record of the sections, which are A, B, and C, that will help us to reach all of the prerequisites for that file.

To help us meet this kind of necessity when we add in the constraint to the current table for the foreign key if the segments that we would like to constrain are going to work or are not listed, we are to use the CREATE INDEX to help file them and at exactly that point utilize the statement of the ADD CONSTRAINT to help add in the needed segments.

Referenced Columns

- The segments that are referenced need to contain some qualities that are unique in their arrangement. This implies that the conditions of REFERENCES needs to work under the same ideas as the two constraints, either the UNIQUE or the PRIMARY KEY, to the table that we are referencing at that time.

For example, the condition that we work with on REFERENCES (C,D), will need to make sure that the PRIMARY KEY or the UNIQUE commands for (C, D) are there in the first place.

- In the REFERENCES provision, in the event that you determine a table yet no sections, CockroachDB will reference back to the key that is essential for this table. In this kind of case, the constraint for the Foreign key will be there, and the essential key must contain a similar amount of sections that you can work with.

Invalid qualities

Single-section foreign keys acknowledge invalid qualities.

Different section (composite) foreign keys just acknowledge invalid qualities in the accompanying situations:

- The compose contains invalid qualities for all of the sections of the foreign keys (if MATCH FULL is determined).

- The compose contains invalid qualities that are there for all of the sections of the foreign key. The COMPOSE command will contain, in this case, invalid qualities for any of the event that happens for one section of the foreign key when the MATCH SIMPLE is determined.

For more data that can help with the foreign keys that are composite, you will need to look back at some of the coordinating segment for that foreign key. Note that allowing some of the invalid qualifies in the referenced sections or the foreign key sections will corrupt some of the integrity present because any key that ends up being invalid will not be checked with that reference table that you set up.

To maintain a strategic distance from all of this, you can work with the command of NOT NULL in order to function with the foreign key while also making some of your existing tables.

We will find that the default is that all of the composite foreign keys will coordinate the command of MATCH SIMPLE to make things happen. However, the MATCH FULL will be accessible whenever it is determined as needed.

When working with the adaptation of the 2.1 and before this, you will find that the main choice seen with this particular key was going to be the MATCH FULL option, but it was done in error. This was a bad thing because it permitted an invalid quality to the sections of our reference keys, and it brought back the wrong and undesired kinds of qualities. This can be done in two main methods, that is:

1. MATCH FULL ought not to permit blended invalid and non-invalid qualities. See underneath for more subtleties on the contrasts between examination strategies.

2. Null qualities can't ever be contrasted with one another.

To help us to handle some of these issues, the key matches that were defined before 19.1 will utilize the examination technique of MATCH SIMPLE. We can also add in some of the capacity in order to figure out both the MATCH SIMPLE and MATCH FULL.

In the event that you have this kind of key constraint and migrated to the version of 19.1, this is the point where we want to double-check that the command of MATCH SIMPLE is going to work for your blueprint and then figure out how this is going to meet your needs.

For some of the purposes of coordinating, composite foreign keys will be found in a certain state, usually one out of three potential possibilities that will include some of the keys that are valid and we can use, the invalid keys that we can't use when we want to do some coordination and some unacceptable keys that we are not able to embed no matter what the means are.

The next command is the MATCH SIMPLE. This MATCH SIMPLE command stipulates that:

• Valid keys have to make sure that all of the qualities are valid.

- Invalid keys contain at least one invalid quality to work with, though it is possible that there are more than that.

- Unacceptable keys will be different because they will have a mix of this command in order to get some of the desired results as well.

For models indicating how the calculations of the key coordination are going to work, you are able to Match up the foreign keys that are composite, included with the commands of MATCH FULL and MATCH SIMPLE.

Foreign key activities

When it is time to add in the constraint that you want with the foreign key, you can control what is going to happen with that obliged segment when the referenced section, or the foreign key, is refreshed or deleted.

Parameter Description

ON DELETE NO ACTION   Default activity. In case you are working with something that has the current references to any key you want to work with being deleted, you will easily find that the exchange is short on the end of the statement.

In this case, the key can be refreshed, as long as the activity of ON UPDATE is taken care of.

ON UPDATE NO ACTION   Default activity. If you are working with this and notice that the references to your chosen key are refreshed, then you will notice that the end of the statement is going to fizzle a bit. This means that the key can be deleted here, but it will depend on the activity of ON DELETE>

3.6 Primary Key Constraint

In the order subtleties table, we have an essential key that comprises of two segments: OrderID and ProductID. This means that if we are working with the key constraints here, then it needs to be done when we are at the level for the table.

Chapter 4:

Union and JOINS of SQL

SQL joins are amazingly valuable. Dissimilar to different sorts of SQL join, we are going to see that this kind of joint will not spend any time coordinating a line from the left source table with some of the lines that are found in the right source table. Instead, it is going to spend time making a brand new table that is virtual and will contain the SQL union of quite a bit of the segments that are found in both of the source tables.

When we focus on the table for the virtual outcomes, the sections that originate from the table on the left will contain the same columns found in that left table. But if we are looking at the lines that originated from the correct source table they are going to come in with the worth that is invalid.

This means that the sections that came from our source table will contain all of the same columns that were in that table. For these particular lines, the sections that were in the left table would then be invalid in the process.

Accordingly, the table coming about because of a union join contains every one of the segments of both of your tables as the source, and the number of lines that it is going to have inside will also be the total number of lines that will be in this new table.

The effects of this kind of join isn't promptly valuable by large; it delivers an outcome table with numerous nulls in it. Be that as it may, it is possible for the programmer to get some helpful data from this kind of union, and you work with the articulation of COALESCE. Take a look at this model.

Assume that you work for an organization that plans and fabricates exploratory rockets. You have a few undertakings in progress. You likewise have a few plan engineers who have aptitudes in various regions. As an administrator, you need to know which representatives, having which abilities, have chipped away at which ventures.

Considering the quantity of SQL JOIN activities accessible, relating information from various tables shouldn't be an issue, paying little heed to the tables' structure. You can believe that if the crude information exists in your database, the whole process of SQL is going to be able to show an important structure.

4.3 SQL Left Join

We are going to take a look at the left join, which is there to help us restore all of the lines that are in our left table. This is going to work whether or not the correct table as a coordinating line.

Assuming that we are trying to work with two different tables, including Table A and Table B. Table A will come with us in four lines that are lines one to four. Then there will be four lines in Table B as well, which will be lines three to six.

At the point where we try to get the two tables joined, then all of the lines that are found in the first one, which is going to be our left table, are going to be remembered along the way, whether or not Table B is going to have that same column in it.

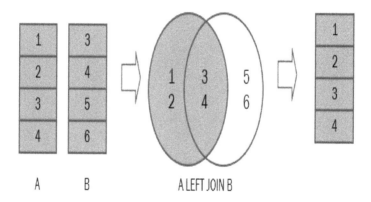

A   B   A LEFT JOIN B

SELECT

A.n

FROM

A

LEFT JOIN B ON B.n = A.n;

The next thing that we can work with is the LEFT JOIN, which will be what shows up when we are done working with the FROM command. The condition that will be able to do this will be known as the join condition in this language.

SQL LEFT JOIN models

SQL LEFT JOIN two table's models

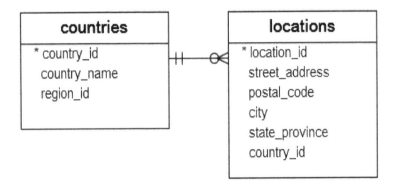

When working with SQL, we are able to utilize the sentence structure to help us combine these two together. The connection between the nations and the tables that we have for areas is going to be one too many. We will combine the country_id segment to the table for the nation.

To look through the names of the nations of China, UK, and US, you would want to work with the syntax below:

SELECT

```
country_id,

country_name

FROM

nations

WHERE

country_id IN ('US', 'UK', 'CN');
```

The accompanying question covers the areas situated in the three countries that we are looking at here. :

```
SELECT

country_id,

street_address,

city

FROM

areas

WHERE

country_id IN ('US', 'UK', 'CN');
```

Now we will utilize the LEFT JOIN statement so that we are able to get the table for the nations to show up at the same table as the areas. The code that we are able to work with here will include:

```
SELECT
```

c.country_name,

c.country_id,

l.country_id,

l.street_address,

l.city

FROM

nations c

LEFT JOIN areas l ON l.country_id = c.country_id

WHERE

c.country_id IN ('US', 'UK', 'CN')

country_name	country_id	country_id	street_address	city
United States of America	US	US	2014 Jabberwocky Rd	Southlake
United States of America	US	US	2011 Interiors Blvd	South San Francisco
United States of America	US	US	2004 Charade Rd	Seattle
United Kingdom	UK	UK	8204 Arthur St	London
United Kingdom	UK	UK	Magdalen Centre, The Oxford Science Park	Oxford
China	CN	NULL	NULL	NULL

We are able to work with the WHERE condition and apply it here so that it is just going to bring out the information that we need from those three main countries.

Since we are working again with that statement of LEFT JOIN, all of the lines that are able to fulfill this condition will show up. For each of the different columns that are able to show up in the nation table we have, we can work with the LEFT JOIN command it will help to find the lines in the area table that match up.

On the off chance that we are not able to find a column that coordinates back, then this will be placed on the new table with the NULL qualities. Since these columns in our new table are going to have these NULL qualities, you can work with the provision of the LEFT JOIN in order to make sure that the whole thing matches up.

SELECT

country_name

FROM

nations c

LEFT JOIN areas l ON l.country_id = c.country_id

WHERE

l.location_id IS NULL

Request BY

country_name;

Another option that we are able to work with is to do a LEFT JOIN with three tables rather than the two that we are talking about before. In order to get started on this, we need to take a look at the tables below.

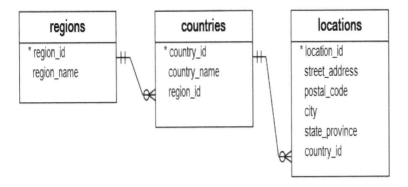

It is possible while we go through this that there is a district that will come with zero nations and then one that has a lot of nations. But it is usually going to be true that each nation is situated in just one locale.

The connection that happens between the locales and the nations will be one too many. Then we can work with the segment of the region_id on the table for nations to help us find the available connections.

Presently you ought to have a decent comprehension of how this command is going to have any effect on the abilities and the functions to the LEFT JOIN statement that we are working with here.

4.4 SQL Right Join

As we work through this we will notice that the RIGHT JOIN is the precise inverse of the LEFT JOIN. It restores all columns that are in the right table and will join together with the lines that we have from our left table to help us get the join condition to meet.

The RIGHT join is a kind of an external join. That is the reason it additionally alludes as right external join. The different varieties of external join are *left join* and *full join*. The accompanying Venn outline delineates how right join functions.

Presently, suppose you need to recover the names of all divisions just as the subtleties of representatives who are working in that office. However, in other circumstance there might be some offices in which no worker is currently working.
The accompanying explanation recovers all the accessible offices just as the id, name, and contracting date of the workers who have a place with that division by joining the representatives and offices tables together utilizing the basic dept_id field.

The right join remembers every one of the lines from the division's table for the outcome set, regardless of whether there is a match on the dept_id segment in the worker's table, as you can unmistakably observe the office "Client care" is incorporated regardless of whether there is no representative in this office.

4.5 SQL Inner Join
The next thing we can work with is the INNER JOIN command. This one chooses all of the lines that show up from both the tables you want to combine, as long as we can find some kind of match within these segments as well.

The SQL INNER JOIN is the same as seen with the statement of JOIN, and it consolidates lines from two tables or more. This kind of join is helpful for bringing together two tables through the specific criteria that we want to set as an administrator

Chapter 5:

The Database

A database is an assortment of data that is sorted out, hence it tends to be effectively gotten to, oversaw and refreshed. PC databases commonly contain accumulations of information records or documents containing data about deals exchanges or associations with explicit clients.

In a relational database, computerized data about a particular client is composed of lines, sections, and some of the tables that we decide to file to make it easier to find the data that is the most pertinent to our work. Interestingly, graph database will work with edges and hubs to help us make those connections and characterize them between information sections and the inquiries. Needless to say, this is going to require that we work with semantic inquiry punctuation.

There are also a few options can offer us Corrosive consistency, which includes strength, detachment, consistency and atomicity, to help ensure that the information we see is reliable and that some of the exchanges we work with are finished.

Different Types of Databases

There have been a lot of advancements when it comes to databases through the years. There are different levels and system databases, in this section, we get to work with ones that are more object-oriented and cloud based or SQL.

In one view, it is possible that the databases can be grouped by the kind of content that they hold onto, which makes it easier for us to work with them and find the one that we need. In figuring, databases are, in some cases, arranged by their hierarchical methodology.

Note that there will be many different types of databases that we are able to work with, starting with the relational database that we work with, all the way to a distributed database, the cloud database, the NoSQL database, and the graph database as well. Let's take a look at how each one is going to work.

First is the relational database. This is one that was designed in 1970, and it is considered one of the best options to work with for many businesses. It will hold onto lots of tables that will place the information you want into some of the predefined classes. Each of these tables in the database will have one information classification in a segment, and each line will also have the right segments.

This kind of database relies on the SQL language that we have been talking about so far. This will be one of the standard client and application program interfaces for this kind of database. Thanks to the extensive features the relational databases, you will find that it is easy to create and work with and it can handle a lot of the great parts that you want in the process.

In addition to working with a relational database, we are able to work with the distributed database, which is a little bit different. This is a type of database where the segments are put into physical areas, and then it will be prepared to be repeated or scattering among various focuses on the system.

You can choose whether to make this database type heterogeneous or homogenous. All of the physical areas that are found in one of these that is more homogenous will have the equivalent basic equipment and will run the right frameworks that needed in order to handle the database application.

Another thing to consider is that the equipment and the database applications in one of the heterogeneous option could be diverse in all of the areas that we are working with. This helps us to get the information in the right places as we go.

The next kind of database that we can work with is the cloud database. This is a database that has been improved or worked on for the virtualized domain. It can either be half of a cloud, a private cloud, or it could be open cloud.

This kind of database is important because it is going to provide you with a ton of advantages. For example, you can pay for the amount of transfer speed and the capacity limit that you are looking for on each of the utilizations that you want along the way, and they are going to provide us with a lot of the versatility that we need for any kind of the databases that we want to work with.

In addition to all of this, the cloud database offers some undertakings the chances to handle applications of a business type as a product of the administration and what it wants to see. Also, it stores that information as needed without pushing it onto your own servers along the way.

Next on the list is the NoSQL database. These are good databases that you can work with, they are valuable for some really big arrangements like when you want to distribute your information. These databases are great when you wish to get information execution that gives results that the relational databases are not able to handle.

These kinds of database are the best when the company using them has to take a bunch of information that is unstructured or information that has been saved in a lot of virtual servers, and needs to be analyzed.

We can also work with some of the object-oriented databases along the way as well. Things that are made when it comes to utilizing object-oriented programming languages are going to be put away into some of the relational databases, but these are the right kinds of databases that we need.

For example, a sight and sound record in our relational databases could end up as an information object that is quantifiable, rather than working with one that is more alphanumeric.

Then there is the graph database as well. This kind of database is graph-oriented, and is somehow similar to the NoSQL database that will work with the graph hypotheses in order to store, guide and then query any of the needed connections. Keep in mind that this kind of database is a big assortment of edges and hubs, and all of the hubs speak to one of the elements, and then the edges speak back to the association that will happen between those hubs.

These graph databases are often not used as much as the others, but they are starting to come into popularity thanks to how they can help with breaking down some of the interconnections that are there.

For example, it is not uncommon for a company to utilize a graph database to help mind information that pertains to their clients from some of the work they do online. It is also common for this kind of database to utilize a language that is known as SPARQL. This language is a bit different, but it allows us to examine graphs and the databases that use them.

5.1 Creating a Database with SQL

Under UNIX, database names are case-touchy (not at all like SQL watchwords), so you should consistently allude to your database as the zoological display, not as Zoo, Zoo, or some other variation. This is likewise valid for table names. (Under Windows, this confinement doesn't have any significant bearing, despite the fact that you should allude to databases and tables utilizing the equivalent letter case all through a given query. In any case, for an assortment of reasons, the prescribed best practice is consistently to utilize the equivalent letter case that was utilized when the database was made.)

Making a database doesn't choose it for use; you should do that unequivocally. To make the zoological display the present database, utilize this announcement:

Your database should be made just once, yet you should choose it to utilize each time you start a MySQL session. You can do this by giving a Utilization articulation as it appeared in the model. On the other hand, you can choose the database on the direct line when you summon MySQL.

Simply indicate its name after any association parameters that you may need to give.

5.2 Removing a database with SQL

With the SQL Server The executive's Studio, you can right tap on the database and select "Erase."

In the erase object window, select the choice "Erase reinforcement and reestablish history data for databases" in the event that you need to evacuate this data.

On the off chance that you need to kick out open associations with your database, select the "Nearby existing associations." It will be difficult to expel the database in the event that you don't choose the last choice, and there are yet open associations with your database. You will get a mistake that the database is still being used and can't be erased

When you hit the alright catch, the database will be evacuated off the SQL example, and the database documents on the operating system level will likewise be expelled. Unquestionably it is important to close down the entire occurrence to evacuate a database.

Presently after the expulsion, despite everything you have some additional cleanup stuff to do that individuals regularly overlook.

Erase the occupations

Erase the occupations that were identified with the database. In the event that you won't expel them, the employments will fall flat, and you will get pointless alarms.

Erase the reinforcement documents

In the event that you need not to bother with the reinforcement documents any longer, simply expel them. I would recommend to keep the last full reinforcement of the database and file it for in any event a year or 2. No one can really tell that someone needs the information later on.

Erase the logins without DB client

Your database had likely some database clients designed that were connected to a server login.

In the event that that server login isn't utilized by other database clients and is somehow still connected to the main server, I would recommend to expel that login. For security reasons as well as to keep your server clean.

5.3 Schema Creation with SQL

A client can make any number of schemas. The schema that has been made has a place with the current client; in any case, it tends to be relegated to another client or job with the ALTER SCHEMA explanation.

The information volume of the items within a schema can be restricted using amounts as in the Schema Portion segment.

When you make another schema, you certainly open this new schema. This implies this new schema is set as the CURRENT_SCHEMA, and any further items made are within it.

If you have specified the alternative IF NOT EXISTS, at that point, no mistake message is tossed if a schema with a similar name currently exists. Likewise, the specified schema is opened regardless of whether it, as of now, exists.

The USING choice in a virtual schema specifies the connector UDF content, which at that point, characterizes the substance of the virtual schema. Using the WITH condition, you can specify certain properties that will be utilized by the connector content.

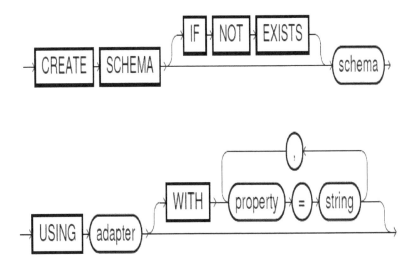

5.4 Creating Tables and Inserting Data into Them

Make a table with the assistance of Make Proclamation.

Model: Make a table titled 'Understudy.'

The linguistic structure is offered underneath to make a table 'Understudy.'

Make TABLE Understudies(Studentid int IDENTITY(1,1) NOT Invalid, Firstname varchar (200) , Lastname varchar (200) , Email varchar (100))

So this linguistic structure will make a table understudy, where the Studentid isn't invalid.

Assume a client needs to embed the information into the table titled 'Understudy.'

Strategy 1: Addition explanation to embed information.

Addition into Students(Studentid,Firstname,lastname, email) Values(1,'Jaya','Singh',)

The aftereffect of this inquiry is verified by using the following question:
Select * FROM Understudies
Strategy 2: Supplement esteems into a table using another table.
Note that we have a table titled 'Understudies,' and we need to embed its qualities into another table titled 'Studentdemo.'

Make table 'Studentdemo.'

Make TABLE Studentsdemo(Studentid int IDENTITY(1, 1) NOT Invalid, Firstname nvarchar (200) , Lastname nvarchar (200) , Email nvarchar (100))

Presently, to embed estimations of table 'Understudies' into table 'Studentsdemo' by using the following articulation.

Addition into
Studentsdemo(Studentid,Firstname,lastname, email)

SELECT Studentid, Firstname, lastname, email FROM Understudies

Aftereffect of this announcement can be verified by using

SELECT * FROM Studentsdemo

Note: To embed the records starting with one table, then onto the next, the information sort of the segment ought to be the same.

5.5 How Tables are Created with SQL

The Make TABLE explanation is utilized to make another table inside one of our databases. The syntax that we are able to use for this one includes:

Make TABLE table_name (

column1 datatype,

column2 datatype,

column3 datatype,

);

The parameters that we are able to use with this one specifies the names that we want to give to the parts of this table.

We can further look at the parameters of the segment and how they are responsible for specifying the information type that we need to find in the segment, or what data the segment can hold onto.

From there, we take a look at making a TABLE model.

The model of the table that we are working with be named "People" and it contains five different parts that we need to focus on: PersonID, LastName, FirstName, Address, and City:

Example

Make TABLE People (

PersonID int,

LastName varchar(255),

FirstName varchar(255),

Address varchar(255),

City varchar(255)

);

5.6 Creating New Tables with SQL Based on Tables Already Existing

A duplicate of an already existing table can be created by using the TABLE command, as long as it's combined with the SELECT command. The new table has a similar segment definition. All sections or specific segments can be chosen. Therefore, when we are making another table with the help of the already existing table, the new table that we want to create would definitely be populated with the qualities that were in that original table.

This is easier to work with than it sound in the beginning, one of the codes that we can use to make it happen is below:

Make TABLE NEW_TABLE_NAME AS

SELECT [column1, column2...columnN]

FROM EXISTING_TABLE_NAME

[WHERE]

5.7 Inserting Data Into a Table with SQL

When we have just a couple of lines of information, the most straightforward way is to include them physically. This by using the Addition proclamation:

Simply put in a few more time auditing the syntax:

- INSERT INTO is the SQL watchword.

- test_results is the name of the table that we need to place the information into.

- VALUES is another SQL catchphrase.

- Then the real information lines will come individually – every one of them among brackets and isolated with commas.

- The field esteems are isolated with commas.

- Watch out for the Content and Date information types in light of the fact that these need to go between punctuations!

- Remember the semicolon at the end of the entire articulation!

5.8 Populating a Table with New Data with SQL

As you most likely are aware, tables that are found in our database of social will denote substances. For example, all of the columns that are found in our table known as Client, will hold onto the information that only goes to that specific client; a line in ORDER_HEADER speaks to an unmistakable request, etc. Ordinarily, the presence of another "reality" element calls for embedding another column. For instance, you would require another line in the Client table if Top, Inc. acquired another client; you have to embed a column into the ORDER_HEADER table when a client makes a request; another line must be added to the Item table if Top begins selling another item, etc.

5.9 Inserting Data into Specific Columns with SQL

The circumstance when you need to embed a line with Invalid qualities for specific segments isn't abnormal. As you most likely are aware, Invalid is utilized when the worth is obscure or non-applicable. For instance, assume you realize Top beginnings selling another item Tidy Timber 30 ×40 ×50, however, we have to remember that some of the properties that are found with this item are still going to be obscure, including the weight and the cost. Because of this, we would want to take the time to record the table known as Item using an Addition articulation.

5.10 Inserting Null Values with SQL

Using the SQL INSERT is also used for the NULL to be inserted into columns.

5.11 Using Order By with SQL

The SQL Request BY provision is utilized to sort the information in rising or diving requests, in view of at least one section. A few databases sort the inquiry brings about a climbing request as a matter of course.

You can utilize more than one segment in the Request BY statement. Ensure whatever segment you are using to sort that segment is in the section list.

5.12 The Where Clause with SQL

There are times when we need to confine the inquiry results to a specified condition. The SQL WHERE statement proves to be useful in such circumstances.

WHERE condition Syntax

The essential syntax for the WHERE condition when utilized in a SELECT articulation is as per the following.

SELECT * FROM table Name WHERE condition;

HERE

• "SELECT * FROM tableName" is the standard SELECT articulation

• "WHERE" is the catchphrase that limits our select inquiry result set, and "condition" is the channel to be applied to the outcomes. The channel could be a range, single esteem, or sub-question.

Assume we need to get a part's close to home subtleties from individuals table given the enrollment number 1; we would utilize the accompanying content to accomplish that.

SELECT * FROM 'individuals' WHERE
'membership_number' = 1;

5.13 DDL in SQL

DDL or Data Definition Language actually comprises of the SQL directions that can be utilized to characterize the database schema. It just manages depictions of the database schema and is utilized to make and modify the structure of database questions in the database.

Instances of DDL directions:

- CREATE – is utilized to make the database or its articles (like a table, file, work, views, store methodology, and triggers).
- DROP – is utilized to erase objects from the database.
- ALTER-is utilized to alter the structure of the database.

5.14 Applying DDL Statements with SQL

SQL's Data Definition Language (DDL) manages the structure of a database. In real sense, it's the Data Control Language, which manages the data contained inside that structure. The DDL comprises of these three affirmations:

CREATE: You utilize the different types of this announcement to fabricate the basic structures of the database.

ALTER: You utilize this announcement to change the structures that you have made.

DROP: You apply this announcement to structures made with the Make articulation, to annihilate them.

Make

You can apply the SQL Make articulation to countless SQL objects, including compositions, spaces, tables, and perspectives. By utilizing the Make Diagram proclamation, you can make a construction, in addition, distinguish its proprietor and indicate a default character set. Here's a case of such an announcement:

Utilize the Make Area explanation to apply imperatives to segment esteems. The limitations applied to a space figure out what protests the area can and can't contain. You can make spaces after setting up a composition.

You make tables by utilizing the Make TABLE explanation, and make it visible utilizing the Make VIEW articulation. When you utilizing the Make TABLE explanation, indicate requirements on the new table's segments simultaneously.

Additionally, you have to Make CHARACTER SET, CREATE Resemblance, and Make Interpretation explanations, which give you the adaptability of making new character sets, gathering groupings, or interpretation tables. (Examination successions characterize the request where you do correlations or sorts. Interpretation tables control the change of character strings starting with one character set then onto the next.)

Change

After making a table, you're not stuck with the exact table for eternity. While using the table, you may find that it's not all that you need it to be. This is where the Modify TABLE articulation comes in to change the table by including changing or erasing a segment in the table. Other than tables, you can also Modify segments and spaces.

DROP

Expelling a table from a database pattern is simple. Simply utilize a DROP TABLE<tablename> proclamation. You delete all data from the table, just as the metadata that characterizes the table in the data lexicon. It's as though the table never existed. You can also use the DROP explanation to dispose of whatever was made by a Make articulation.

5.15 Running the DDL Script in SQL

You can import Cache SQL DDL content documents using either the Store() strategy intelligently from a Terminal session, or the DDLImport("CACHE") technique as foundation work. This strategy can import and execute various SQL directions, allowing you to use a text content document to characterize tables, view and fill them with data. For further subtleties, allude to the Bringing in SQL Code section of this guide.

In the event that you are relocating tables from another merchant's social database to Caché, you may have at least one DDL content inside content records. Caché gives a few %SYSTEM.SQL strategies to help burden such DDL contents into Caché. You can use the universally useful DDLImport() strategy or the %SYSTEM.SQL technique for the particular merchant. The merchant explicit SQL is changed over to Caché SQL and executed. Blunders and unsupported highlights are recorded in log documents. For further subtleties, allude to the Code Movement: Bringing in non-Caché SQL in the "*Bringing in SQL Code*" section of this guide.

For instance, to stack a Prophet DDL record from the Caché order line:

- Start a Terminal session using the Terminal order in the "Caché Block" menu.
- Switch to the namespace on which you wish to stack the table definitions.
- Invoke the ideal DDL import technique and pursue the bearings showed at the terminal.

5.16 Data Manipulation Language

When working with one of these languages, we recognize them as a group of scripts that will include directions so that the client has all of the control they need over the database and the data. Some of the control that they will have includes: embedding the data in their tables, recovering or erasing data on their tables and making changes to that data if they like.

DML is usually fused together with the databases that use SQL.

DML resembles the English language and upgrades productive client association with the framework. The utilitarian ability of DML is sorted out in control directions like SELECT, UPDATE, Supplement INTO and Erase FROM, as explained below:

1. SELECT: This is the direction used to recover some lines out of the table. It is the most popular in DML therefore the SQL part of it works.
2. UPDATE: This is the command that adjusts the data of one record. It makes it easier to add in the changes that we want to see in our databases.
3. INSERT: This is the command that adds in new records to the database.
4. DELETE: This final command is the one that takes one or more record out of the database and deletes them permanently.

Chapter 6:

Logins, Users, Roles, and Functions

Logins exist in the ace database, put away in sysxlogins. Think about a login as

something that enables a client to interface with the server, yet not to get to any

specific database. You can have a 'SQL' login, which is a login name in addition to a secret word, or you can utilize NT/confided in security, where you include either an NT client or bunch name as a login. Without jumping profoundly into which you should utilize, simply remember that you must have a login to associate with the server and, that it is put away in the ace database.

Making a client in a database gives a login authorization to get to that database. On the off chance that you use Undertaking Director, you'll see that the drop-down list for including clients comprises of all the logins that exist on that server. Clients are put away in that database, not in the ace database. This bodes well if you consider what happens when you disconnect the database - the clients remain inside the MDF. When you reattach the MDF to an alternate server, the clients are still there.

However, the logins may not be.

You regularly handle consents by making jobs - think about an NT gathering. You ought to consistently allocate authorizations to a job, not to a client.

When there is another database that needs the primary client set up, you need to do the following:

- Either re-utilize a current login or make another login.
- Add a job to the database
- Add the client to the database.
- Add the client to the job you just made.
- Assign consents to the job.

6.1 Server Logins

Logins are related to clients by the security identifier (SID). A login is required for access to the SQL server. The way to check that a specific login is legitimate is designated "confirmation." This login must be related to a SQL Server database client. You utilize the client record to control exercises performed in the database. On the off chance that no client account exists in a database for a particular login, the client that is utilizing that login can't get to the database despite the fact that the client might have the option to associate with SQL Server. The single special case to this circumstance is the point at which the database contains the "visitor" client account. A login that doesn't have a related client account is mapped to the visitor client. On the other hand, if a database client exists, yet there is no login related, the client can't sign into SQL Server.

6.2 Server Level Roles

SQL Server gives server-level jobs to help when dealing with the consents on a server. These jobs are security principals gathering different principals. Server-level jobs are server-wide in the scope of their consent. (Jobs resemble bunches in the Windows working framework.)

Fixed server jobs are accommodated comfort and in reverse similarity. Relegate progressively explicit consents at whatever point conceivable.

SQL Server gives nine fixed server jobs. The consents that are conceded to the fixed server jobs (aside from open) can't be changed. Starting with SQL Server 2012 (11.x), you can make client characterized server jobs and add server-level consents to the client characterized server jobs.

You can include server-level principals (SQL Server logins, Windows records and Windows gatherings) into server-level jobs. Every individual from a fixed server job can add different logins to that equivalent job. Individuals from client characterized server jobs can't add other server principals to the job.

The accompanying table shows the fixed server-level jobs and their capacities.

Fixed server-level role	Description
sysadmin	This includes some members that have a fixed role in the sever and will not change.
Server admin	The members in this category have a great role, and they can also change the options of the whole server or even shut down what is happening on the server.
Security admin	The members in this category are responsible for handling all of the logins on the system and their properties. They can either revoke, deny or grant permissions on what to happen on both the database and the server level. In addition, they can reset the passwords used on the server. One thing to remember here is that the ability to add in some access to the engine of the database and to configure some of the permissions

	allows the admin of security to assign most of the permissions as well.
Process admin	Members in this category have the role of ending any processes that are going on in the database, putting a stop to it all.
Setup admin	The members in this group are be able to add and take away any of the servers that are found in this process with the help of the command of Transact-SQL
Bulk admin	The members in this category handle the statement of BULK INSERT.
Disk admin	This is the category tasked with the role of managing the files on the disk to keep them organized and ready to go.
Db creator	Members in this group are responsible for carrying out different roles including creating, dropping, altering and restoring.

Public	All of the logins of this server belong to the public server. When the principal of the server has not been denied or granted specific permission on an object, then the user can take on the permissions that are found by the public. We only want to assign this kind of permission on an object that is easily accessible to all. We will not change over the membership to the public.
	Note: The public part receives a different type of implementation that is not the same as the other roles. Whereby we can grant, deny and revoke the permissions on the server roles that are fixed in this section.

6.3 Database Users

Database clients are the people who truly utilizes and take advantage of the database. There will be various sorts of clients relying on the database based on their needs.

1. Application Software engineers - They are the designers who cooperate with the database by methods for DML inquiries. These DML inquiries are written in

application programs like C, C++, JAVA, Pascal and so on. These questions are changed over into object code to speak with the database. For instance, composing a C program to create the report of representatives who are working specifically in the office will include a question to bring the information from the database. It will incorporate an installed SQL inquiry in the C Program.

2. Sophisticated Clients - They are database designers, who compose SQL questions to choose/embed/erase/update information. They don't utilize any application or projects demanding the database. They legitimately communicate with the database by means of question language like SQL. These clients will be researchers, engineers, experts who completely study SQL and DBMS to apply the ideas in their prerequisites. To put it plainly, we can say this class incorporates architects and engineers of DBMS and SQL.

3. Specialized Clients - These are additionally modern clients, yet they compose uncommon database application programs. They are the designers who build up the intricate projects to the necessity.

4. Stand-alone Clients - These clients will have a stand-alone database for their own

utilization. These sorts of database will have readymade database bundles which will have menus and graphical interfaces.

5. Native Clients - these are the clients who utilize the current application to collaborate with the database. For instance, online library framework, ticket booking frameworks, ATMs and so forth which has existing applications and clients use them to interface with the database to satisfy their solicitations.

6.4 Database Level Roles

Database-level jobs are database-wide in the scope of their authorization.

In order to add and expel clients to a database job, use the Include Part and DROP Part choices of the Change Job proclamation. Parallel Information Stockroom doesn't bolster this utilization of Adjust Job. Utilize the more seasoned sp_addrolemember and sp_droprolemember strategies.

There are two kinds of database-level jobs: *fixed-database jobs* that are predefined in the database and *client characterized database jobs* that you can make.

Fixed-database jobs are characterized at the database level and exist in every database. Individuals from the db_owner database job can oversee fixed-database job enrollment. There are additionally some particular reason database jobs in the msdb database.

You can include any database account and other SQL Server jobs into database-level jobs.

The consents of client characterized database jobs can be altered by utilizing the Award, DENY, and Disavow articulations. For more data, see Consents (Database Motor).

For a listing of the considerable number of consents, see the Database Motor Authorizations blurb. (Server-level authorizations can't be conceded to database jobs. Logins and other server-level principals, *(for example, server jobs)* can't be added to database jobs. For server-level security in SQL Server, use server jobs. Server-level consents can't be allowed through jobs in SQL Database and SQL Information Distribution center.)

Fixed-Database Jobs

These jobs exist in all databases. With the exception of the open database job, the authorizations appointed to the fixed-database jobs can't be changed.

6.5 Like Clause

The SQL LIKE provision is used to contrast an incentive with comparable qualities utilizing special case administrators. There are two trump cards utilized related to the LIKE administrator.

- The percent sign (%)
- The underscore (_)

The percent sign speaks to zero, one or different characters. The underscore speaks to a solitary number or character. These images can be utilized in blends.

6.6 SQL Functions

SQL has many functions in capacities for performing counts on information.

SQL Total Capacities

SQL total capacities return a solitary worth, determined from values in a section.

Valuable total capacities:

- AVG() - Returns the normal worth

- COUNT() - Returns the quantity of lines

- FIRST() - Returns the principal esteem

- LAST() - Returns the last worth

- MAX() - Returns the biggest worth

- MIN() - Returns the littlest worth

- SUM() - Returns the aggregate

SQL Scalar capacities

SQL scalar capacities return a solitary worth, in light of the info esteem.

Valuable scalar capacities:

- UCASE() - Changes over a field to capitalized
- LCASE() - Changes over a field to bring down case
- MID() - Concentrate characters from a book field
- LEN() - Returns the length of a book field
- ROUND() - Rounds a numeric field to the quantity of decimals determined
- NOW() - Returns the present framework date and time
- FORMAT() - Configurations how a field is to be shown

6.7 SQL AVG Function

The function SQL AVG is used when an expression's average is returned within the SELECT statement.

6.8 SQL Round Function

The SQL ROUND function is used for accurate number rounding.

6.9 SQL SUM Function

The function SUM in SQL Server is able to calculate an expression's specific values and sums.

6.10 SQL Max Function

The function MAX in SQL Server is to calculate the value of the maximum returns of sets.

As observed before, there are a lot of different parts that show up when working with some of the parts of the database, especially when we work with the idea of SQL and what it can do.

Chapter 7:

How SQL Views are Created

Views in SQL are somewhat virtual tables. A view also has lines and sections similar to a real table in the database. We can make a view by choosing fields from at least one of tables present in the database. A View can either have every one of the columns of a table or explicit lines dependent on certain conditions.

7.1 How to Add a View to a Database

First make a database view to join tables. Then you can make a report dependent on the database view.

1. Create a database view: *Make the database view.*

2. Add a table to the database view: *Determine the table to join to the database view.*

3. Specify a field to return: *Utilize the View Field structure to limit or determine a field that you need to be returned by the joined table.*

4. Relabel a section: *Now and again, two distinct tables may have fields of a similar name that are both significant, (for example, two tables with a*

sys_updated_on field). You should rename one of these fields.

5. Specify the number of records to return: *Indicate the number of records to return for a database view.*

6. Test the database view: *Check that the database view works effectively.*

7.2 How to Create an Updateable View

Updatable implies that a view can be a piece of an UPDATE, a Supplement or an Erase articulation.

To be updatable, all the various records inside of this view should be balanced association with the records in the hidden tables.

7.3 How to Drop a View

To help us get rid of one of the views we have from a particular database, we just need to work with the DROP VIEW command. In this linguistic structure, you indicate the name of the view that you need to drop after the DROP VIEW keywords. In case the view has a location mapping also determine the name of the pattern to which the view has a place.

In the event that you choose to expel a view that doesn't exist, SQL Server will give an error message. The IF EXISTS condition keeps an error from happening when you erase a view that doesn't exist.

7.4 Database Security

When referring to database security, we're talking about collective measures that are utilized to secure and protect databases or the management software of a database from any uses that are either malicious or illicit attacks or threats.

This term is very broad and involves many different methods and tools allows security to be maintained throughout the database's landscape.

7.5 The Security Model of SQL

The SQL Server Security model has a great features to it. A few of my companions are experts in it as it is their essential capacity on the DBA group they work for. My companion (and as of late printed Information Stage MVP) Kenneth Fisher (b|t).

Don't fret; once you get the key ideas it gets simpler.

Conclusion

There you have it, a complete beginner's introduction to SQL programming and all of the fascinating functions that come with it.

Hopefully, you got a lot out of this book and each chapter and will further your understanding of

SQL.

The faster you get a grasp on SQL and how data and databases play a major role in the world of programming, the sooner you'll see yourself advancing through the language and eventually being able to complete more complex tasks.

Now, all you need to do is give this book a great Amazon review so that others can also have a heads up on what a great read SQL Programming really is.

-

CPSIA information can be obtained
at www.ICGtesting.com
Printed in the USA
BVHW091406220221
600766BV00013B/1101